FINER
THAN GOLD

JAMES ROBINSON

FINER
THAN GOLD

SAINTS AND RELICS IN THE MIDDLE AGES

THE BRITISH MUSEUM PRESS

In memory of Maureen Greenwood

© 2011 The Trustees of the British Museum

James Robinson has asserted the right to be identified
as the author of this work.

First published in 2011 by The British Museum Press
A division of The British Museum Company Ltd
38 Russell Square, London WC1B 3QQ

www.britishmuseum.org

ISBN 978 0 7141 2822 1

Frontispiece: Detail of the Holy Thorn reliquary (see pp. 58–61).
Opposite: Reliquary pendant of St Demetrios with St George (see pp. 82–6).

Designed by Maggi Smith at Sixism
Printed in China by Toppan Leefung Printing Ltd

The papers used in this book are recyclable products and the manufacturing
processes are expected to conform to the environmental regulations of the
country of origin.

CONTENTS

ACKNOWLEDGEMENTS

Grateful thanks are extended to the following for their assistance, advice, support and understanding during the authorship and production of this book: Coralie Hepburn, Jonathan Williams, John Cherry, Leslie Webster, Dora Thornton, Giulia Bartram, Anna Harnden, Naomi Speakman, Chloe Luxford, Saul Peckham, John Williams, Jenny Ramkalawon, Axelle Russo, Melanie Morris, Maggi Smith, Laura Lappin, Catherine Hall and Stuart Mann.

PREFACE

THE CULT OF THE SAINTS is one of the identifying characteristics of the Middle Ages, which are generally understood to cover the thousand or so years between the collapse of Rome (around 496) and the dawn of the Renaissance. The period is commonly perceived as a time of illiteracy, pestilence, religious repression and superstition. Consequently the medieval Christian belief in the miracle-working power of saints' relics has often been dismissed as gullible nonsense without any clear understanding of its rich material history, highly sophisticated system of symbolism and strong political resonances. This book will seek to shed light on the cult of the saints by looking in more detail at the wonderful works of art that were produced to contain relics, the extensive pilgrimage routes that connected medieval Europe, and the individuals whose political power was strengthened by their personal relic collections.

When Polycarp, bishop of Smyrna in Turkey, was martyred in about 156, his followers collected his bones, which were considered to be 'more valuable than precious stones and finer than refined gold'.[1] The account that details this event goes on to describe the respect that was customarily paid to those who had died for their faith. Once Polycarp's bones were secured in a suitable place, the anniversary of his martyrdom could be duly celebrated. This practice had its origins in the funerary rites of the pagan Roman world, when at intervals throughout the year memorial feasts would take place for the dead. Ultimately it evolved into the annual celebration of saints' feast days that remains familiar to many of us today.

Fig. 1
Relics of St Thérèse of Lisieux

The relics of St Thérèse of Lisieux venerated at
Portsmouth Cathedral, 16 September 2009.

Contemporary devotion to the saints still forms a vital part of
religious life for vast numbers of people, as was demonstrated in the
United Kingdom between September and October 2009 when the
relics of St Thérèse of Lisieux were sent to various venues around
the country [fig. 1]. Large crowds amassed at each place in a manner
that must have resembled the emotive gatherings which surrounded
medieval shrines. In an increasingly secular age, the saint's ability to
harness faith has been employed on a flamboyantly modern world
tour that started in 1997, the hundredth anniversary of Thérèse's death.
The appreciation of the power of relics that has propelled the tour is
intrinsically medieval in origin and it is precisely this spiritual force,
thought to reside in the physical remains of saints, in objects they
have touched or owned, or in spaces they have occupied, that this
book will explore.

The first saints, such as Polycarp, were early Christian martyrs
who had suffered terrible deaths under the various persecutions of
the Roman era. These began in earnest in 64 under Emperor Nero
(reigned 54–68) and continued intermittently until the Edict of Milan

in 313, when Christianity was made legal under Emperor Constantine (reigned 306–337). The word 'martyr' comes from the Greek word for 'witness', and was applied to those who refused to relinquish their faith in the face of torture and death. The theologian Tertullian (d. c. 220–25) converted to Christianity as a direct consequence of observing the willing acceptance of death by Christians. He wrote the *Apologeticum* in 197 as a defence of Christianity to the provincial governors of the Roman Empire. His concluding remark that 'we multiply the more we are mown down by you: the blood of Christians is seed' judged that the persecutions only succeeded in increasing the numbers of Christians.[2] The brutalized and often dismembered bodies of the martyrs were gathered up and treasured as sacred by their fellow Christians, and were seen as tangible links with the divine: through their glorious deaths, the martyrs had secured a place at the side of Christ in heaven. From this position they were able to petition Christ with prayers on behalf of mankind who worshipped at tombs still imbued with their presence. With the Edict of Milan, Christians were free to practise their religion under Roman rule. They rapidly sought out the graves of the martyrs, regarding the ground itself as sanctified, and built churches over them that were frequently dedicated to the saint in question.

The value attached to the body of a saint is demonstrated by events following the death of St Francis of Assisi on 3 October 1226. The next day his funeral procession from nearby Porziuncola to Assisi passed the convent of San Damiano, the home of the Franciscan order of Poor Clares, to allow St Clare and her nuns to see the body. He was then taken to the church of San Giorgio where he was buried with an

Fig. 2
The Funeral of St Francis, **Sassetta**
Siena, 1437–44
Egg tempera on poplar, 88.4 x 53.5 cm

This panel from an altarpiece dedicated to St Francis was commissioned for the church of San Francesco in Borgo Sansepolcro. It shows the ceremony surrounding the burial of a saint.

The National Gallery, London

appropriate degree of ritual [fig. 2]. At the time of his canonization in 1228 the foundation stone was laid for a new church in Assisi dedicated in his name. His body was taken there in 1230, whereupon it was buried again beneath the high altar and sealed with stone in an attempt to prevent any relics from being stolen. In the fourth century the fear that his body might be disinterred prompted St Anthony to forbid his followers from revealing the location of his grave. These two examples demonstrate the longstanding enthusiasm for relic collecting, but also reflect co-existent concerns about the ethics of violating the bodies of the dead.

The Middle Ages may be justly characterized as the period that invented and developed to an extraordinary degree the veneration of saints' relics, but it was also an age of great dialectic when ideas were rigorously debated. Guibert of Nogent (1055–1124) was highly critical of the practice of relic veneration in his work *De sanctis et eorum pigneribus* (*On the Saints and their Relics*), citing the elaborate decoration of shrines as a means of fooling the naive. His near contemporary, Thiofrid of Echternach (d. 1110), who wrote the treatise *Flores epytaphii sanctorum* (*Flowers Strewn over the Tombs of the Saints*) between about 1098 and 1105, argued eloquently that the richness of the reliquary was made valuable only by the relic it contained. It is Thiofrid's understanding that prevailed for most in the period covered in this book.

HOLY PLACES 1

SAINT, SHRINE AND CITY

Fig. 3
St Helena finding the True Cross
Northern Italy, *c*. 825
Parchment, 53 x 27.2 x19 cm
(without bindings)

In this detail from a compendium of
canon law, St Helena is shown receiving
the True Cross. Below, the Cross is
excavated with the crosses of the
two thieves crucified with Christ.

Biblioteca Capitolare, Vercelli

ONSTANTINE'S LEGALIZATION of Christianity in 313 brought with it a significant and paradoxical dilemma. The foundation of early Christian churches relied heavily upon the very concept of martyrdom and the power of saints' bones to endow the buildings with their intrinsic, sacred qualities. With an end to the persecution of the Christians, the principal source of relics was gone. Gradually, however, a means of obtaining new relics emerged. The most significant development in this process was undoubtedly the legendary discovery of the True Cross in Jerusalem by Constantine's mother, the Empress Helena (*c*. 246/50–330) [fig. 3].

St Helena – sacred archaeologist

Helena's early life is shrouded in mystery and speculation. The *History of the Kings of Britain* by Geoffrey of Monmouth (*c*. 1100–1155), composed around 1136, describes her as Elaine, the daughter of King Cole, fixing her origins in Essex. Today she remains commemorated as the patron saint for the town of Colchester, whose civic regalia include a coat of arms bearing an image of the True Cross. She is now more widely believed to be from the ancient Roman province of Bithynia in modern-day Turkey. Constantine's affection and reverence for his mother is reflected in the design of coins minted in her name [fig. 4]. From the time of Constantine's assumption of complete power over the empire in 324, Helena's title changed from 'nobilissima femina' ('most noble lady') to 'augusta' ('empress'). After her death *c*. 330, she was given a new distinction – that of saint. Devotion to St Helena was widespread throughout the Middle Ages, when her position of empress

Figs 4 and 5
Two coins with a bust of the Empress Helena on the obverse
Above: Sirmium (present-day Sremska Mitrovica, Serbia), *c*. 324–5, gold, D 2 cm
Below: England, 6th or 7th century, gold, D 1.9 cm

The British Museum, London

IUDAS

UBI IUDA
S CRUCE IHU
HIT

Fig. 6
The Psalter map
England, c. 1262
Parchment, c. 14.5 x 10 cm

Jerusalem is depicted at the centre of the earth
in a perception of the world influenced by the
Bible. The upper part of the map shows Asia
and the lower half is divided into quarters
representing Africa and Europe.

The British Library, London

carried with it almost as much mystique as her saintly status. As late
as the sixth or seventh century, imitation coins based on those minted
in Helena's lifetime were used for their amuletic properties [fig. 5].

In about 326 Helena embarked on a pilgrimage to the Holy Land,
determined to locate the sites where Christ's infancy, ministry and
Passion had unfolded. Her quest was successful and resulted
furthermore in the discovery of a number of relics allegedly associated
with Christ's Passion, including the Cross from the Crucifixion.
Helena's travels were to transform the landscape of the territories she
explored through her legendary foundation of numerous churches in
places connected with the life of Christ. Each of them was to become
the focus of pilgrimage. Among the principal attractions was the Church
of the Holy Sepulchre in Jerusalem, constructed on the site of Christ's
Resurrection [fig. 7]. Jerusalem was considered to be the centre of the
Christian world, a perception drawn from the biblical commentaries
of Jerome. Jerome interpreted the description in Psalm 73 of salvation
occurring in the middle of the earth by referring to a passage in
Ezekiel (5:5), which states: 'I have placed Jerusalem in the middle of
the peoples, and around her the lands.' This world view was reflected
in medieval maps, which were designed for instruction rather than
navigation and attempted to condense the Christian cosmos [fig. 6].
The world, with the east at the top, is visualized as a circle supported
by two dragons, above which Christ prays between two angels.

Jerusalem's significance in medieval belief was manifold. It was
understood that Golgotha, where the Crucifixion took place, was also
the precise spot where Adam was buried, thus making a very direct

Fig. 7
The Church of the Holy Sepulchre
Jerusalem

link between the Fall from Paradise and the sacrifice offered by Christ to atone for mankind's sins. Additionally, as the setting for Christ's Passion, Jerusalem was generally identified as the likely location for the Second Coming. Helena's desire to feel close to the events in the Gospels represents a wider human impulse to feel a physical connection with past happenings, but she was also looking forward to the future and seeking safety for her soul on the Day of Judgement.

Others quickly followed in Helena's footsteps. The female ascetic, Egeria, who visited the Holy Land in the 380s, kept a detailed account of her travels, describing her veneration of the relic of the True Cross on Good Friday and the security measures in place to protect it. On her travels through Palestine, Syria and Egypt, Egeria collected her own modest relics, including fruit and twigs. The commonly held notion that prompted her gathering of such items was that the holiness of Christ, his disciples, saints and prophets had left a lasting imprint on the environment they once occupied, and that any trace of this sacred power could translate into material and spiritual benefits. Gregory of Tours (c. 538–94), who wrote a compilation of miracle stories, Glory of the Martyrs, between about 585 and 588, reveals his understanding of this phenomenon when he describes the scene at the Holy Sepulchre:

Marvellous power appears from the tomb where the Lord's body lay. Often the ground is covered with a natural radiant brightness; then it is sprinkled with water and dug up, and from it tiny [clay] tokens are shaped and sent to the different parts of the world. Often ill people acquire cures by means of

Fig. 8
Reliquary cross
Probably Constantinople
(present-day Istanbul), early 11th century
Gold and enamel, H 6.1 cm

The front plate of this cross, allegedly
found on the site of the Great Palace of
Constantinople, is missing. The reverse,
shown here, represents the Virgin Mary
with St Basil and St Gregory Thaumaturgus.
It is likely that the reliquary was made to
contain a relic of the True Cross.

The British Museum, London

these tokens ... But what do I dare to say about them, since
faith believes that everything that the sacred body touched
is holy?[3]

The distillation of divine power into relics meant that the holiness of
cities such as Jerusalem was essentially portable. Their circulation from
the Holy Land ensured that even distant communities could share in
the sensation of greater closeness to Christ.

Constantinople – seat of power

Given the great power invested in relics, it was perfectly natural for
Helena to send a sizeable piece of the True Cross to her son, the
emperor. Constantine's decision in 324 to consolidate the empire by
moving from Rome to Byzantium found him with a city lacking the
superabundance of martyrs' remains that had characterized the former
capital. He renamed the city Constantinople and, with the help of his
mother, began to secure its welfare by stockpiling relics of the highest
order. This process was continued by subsequent emperors until
Constantinople had no earthly parallel in the number of relics it
possessed. Along with the fragment of the True Cross, Helena apparently
sent home the nails from the Crucifixion, which she had discovered at
the same time. She had one set into Constantine's diadem and two into
the bridle of his horse. It was long believed that the diadem was placed
by Constantine on a statue of himself so that, according to Gregory of
Tours, 'a helmet of salvation crowns the entire fortification over which
it towers'.[4] Other authorities claimed that the same statue also enclosed

an assortment of relics, including that of the True Cross. The rationale behind this putative placement of relics was that they would offer more potent protection than any mere material structure. This conviction prompted a veritable frenzy of relic collecting over successive generations as the imperial palace and each new foundation was equipped with remains of truly astounding provenance. The bodies of the apostles Timothy, Andrew and Luke were brought to the Church of the Holy Apostles, probably by Constantine's son, Constantius II (317–61), in 356 and 357. Their positioning in a church reserved for imperial burials was a deliberate attempt to connect dynastic succession with apostolic heritage. Other holy bodies followed: in 406 the relics of the prophet Samuel, and in 415 the bodies of John the Baptist's father, Zacharias, and Joseph, the son of Jacob. The rich repository of relics at the command of the emperor placed him in an enviable position of strength and Constantinople became an important centre for the diffusion of relics. Queen Radegund of Poitiers (d. 587) petitioned Emperor Justin II (d. 578) for a relic of the True Cross, which he dispatched with others for deposit in her convent in 569. The convent was subsequently renamed the Abbey of the Holy Cross and became a pilgrimage destination of some local significance.

The wood of the True Cross was perhaps the most highly valued of all relics, serving as a stirring reminder of Christ's sacrifice, enriched by contact with his broken and bleeding body. For its veneration it was set into suitably beautiful reliquaries that would mostly incorporate the shape of the cross in their design and might provide some additional embellishment in the form of narrative scenes. The front and back of a

cross that survive in the British Museum and the Kunstgewerbemuseum in Berlin may have been designed to ornament such a reliquary [figs 9 and 10]. They were produced in the Meuse Valley between about 1160 and 1170, and combine the sophisticated use of imagery with a supreme mastery of the enameller's craft. A richly varied palette of enamels is laid onto plaques of gilt copper alloy with settings for rock crystal, lapis lazuli, garnet and amethyst. Each terminal of the cross and its central plaque is decorated with a narrative that refers to the sacrifice of Christ. The scenes that are generally considered to form the front of the cross are drawn from the Old Testament, but were understood by a medieval audience to symbolize or anticipate Christ's Crucifixion. At the centre, Jacob blesses Joseph's sons, Ephraim and Manasseh, forming a cross with his arms. Above, Moses and Aaron observe the brazen serpent on its column, the antithesis of the true deity of Christ on the Cross. The left terminal shows the widow of Sarepta forming a cross with two sticks and the right depicts the Passover where the slaughtered lamb serves as a symbol of Christ, the Lamb of God. Below, Caleph and Joshua bear grapes from the Promised Land. The reverse panels tell the story of Helena's discovery of the True Cross. The left terminal describes how Helena located Golgotha, the site of Christ's Crucifixion, through the interrogation of a Jew, Judas Cyriacus; Judas yields his secret knowledge under trial by fire on the right terminal. The excavation of Golgotha revealed three crosses, shown on the bottom panel: that of Christ and the two thieves executed with him. In the central scene the identity of the True Cross is verified through its resurrection of a man from the dead, and, in the top terminal, Helena venerates the Cross on an altar.

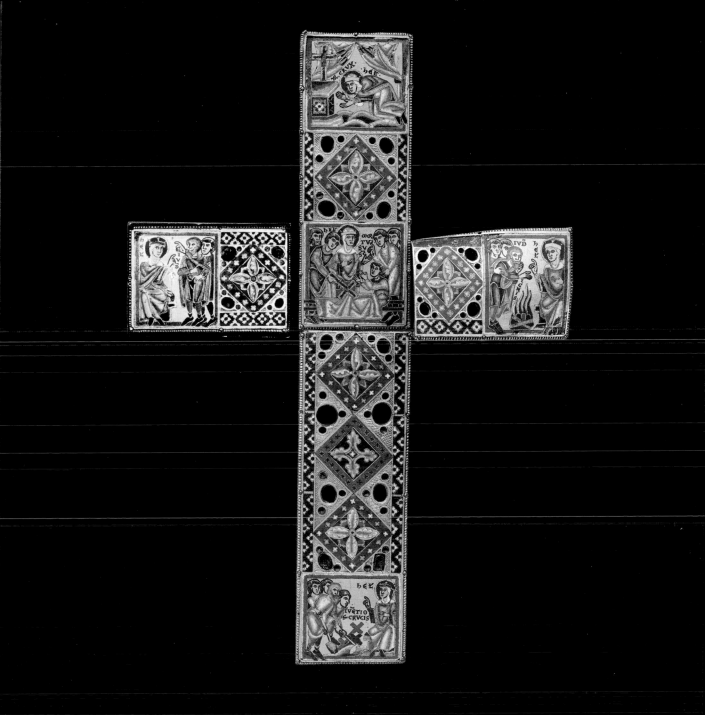

Abu Mina – expanding horizons

Helena's activities as pilgrim and church builder along with the
continuing patronage of the imperial court gave great impetus to
the process of pilgrimage throughout the Mediterranean world. In
Egypt from the fifth century onwards the cult of St Menas at Abu
Mina close to Alexandria attracted large crowds of pilgrims seeking
miraculous cures at the saint's shrine. Descriptions from the time
of Emperor Justinian (527–65) provide a glimpse of the large-scale
complex that arose at Abu Mina, where hostels, shops and public
baths catered for the steady flow of pilgrims. An indication of the
volume of visitors who travelled there is given by the very considerable
number of pilgrims' flasks that survive bearing the saint's image [fig.
11]. The terracotta flasks, mass manufactured in moulds, were
made to contain miracle-working water or oil that flowed at the
shrine. The front of the flasks most usually show St Menas's standard
iconography of the saint with his arms outstretched in prayer, standing
between two kneeling camels. The camels relate to the legend of his
entombment whereby the patriarch of Alexandria was instructed by
a vision to convey the saint's body to the desert. At a certain point
the camels transporting the body refused to travel any further and
this was taken as a sign that the burial spot had been reached. The
reverse of the illustrated example from the British Museum shows
a ship at sea, which probably reflects the safe passage that the saint
assured to pilgrims visiting the shrine. The widespread popularity
of the saint's cult is demonstrated by the large distribution of the
pilgrims' flasks.

In Rome, at the church of St Paul Outside-the-Walls, a chapel was dedicated to St Menas where, reportedly, a small carved ivory container was found [fig. 12]. Although circular boxes of this type were most usually made to store cosmetics or medicine, they were also used as reliquaries. This example may even have transported relics of Menas from Alexandria to Rome. It is carved with great skill and subtlety with scenes from the saint's life. The execution of Menas, who was apparently martyred under Emperor Diocletian (c. 244–311) in about 295, is depicted on one side. He kneels before a Roman official with his hands bound while the executioner raises his sword; behind appears an angel to carry away the saint's soul. On the other side, Menas stands within an arcade, flanked by pilgrims soliciting his aid.

Fig. 12
Pyxis
Probably Alexandria, 6th century
Ivory, H 7.9 cm D 11.9 cm

Scenes from the life of St Menas are depicted around this circular box. They include his judgement, execution and veneration as a saint.

The British Museum, London

Pilgrimage – penance and reward

The distribution of relics was key to the development of pilgrimage routes since shrines depended on the miracle-working agency that they offered. By the close of the Middle Ages an extensive network had grown with an infrastructure to support it that included funding provision, hospitals (or hostels) to supply care and lodging, and the manufacture of souvenirs such as badges and printed pictures. There were, of course, many hazards to be met and long-distance travellers might run the risk of encountering brigands, shipwreck, disease and even death, or find themselves in a war-zone accused of spying. A detailed knowledge of the terrain was desirable and this might be provided by local guides. Bernard of Angers, writing in the early eleventh century, describes how

gebon.

azropol castri

Mone sepult

Mons ph cor

Ser

Galgala vbi filij ihrl transito ordane diu morabant

locy vbi decapitatu fuit Jacoby minor

day joh ewnte

Palaciu qd xpianis constructu et palaciu dauid appellant

Hospitale inqp egni ftima venetes reportata

teplu symeonis

domg anne

Templu Salomois

CIVITAS · IHERVSALEM

locy vbi xpoth mab anglm accepit diem ergo mana assumet in celu

Porta Eradio se apta fuit ingemo

aurea p Imparu Et hodie qum id lit

Spelnca vbi xpus orauit in orto

Sepulchru marie virgi

vbi lignu ste crucis iacuit

Torrens cedron

Peter Le Puy had moved to the eastern Mediterranean and made a living
as a guide and interpreter there: 'He knew the land and sea routes, the
public roads, the ports of call, the side roads and the customs of the
people and their language.'[5] With the advent of printing in Europe from
the mid-fifteenth century, published accounts of pilgrimages began to
be circulated. The first was a book produced in Germany in 1486
inspired by a visit to the Holy Land that detailed some of the places,
people and wildlife that could be seen by pilgrims on their way to
Jerusalem [fig. 13]. Entitled *Peregrinatio in terram sanctam* (*Travels to the
Holy Land*), it constitutes the earliest known printed travel guide and
proved enormously popular, running to twelve editions in several
languages between 1486 and 1522. It was compiled by Bernard von
Breydenbach (1440–97), who travelled with Johann, Duke of Solms-
Lich, and Philip von Bicken between 1483 and 1484. An artist, Erhard
Reeuwich, accompanied the pilgrims to keep a visual record of the trip.
He included views of Venice, Rhodes, Heraklion and Jerusalem, along
with representations of a woman in Venetian costume, figures in
'Saracen' dress, and depictions of animals such as a giraffe, a camel
and a crocodile.

The hardship endured on pilgrimage was considered to be a
measure of the pilgrim's devotion and was factored into calculations of
the merit that was accrued as a consequence of the trip. In the case of
penitential pilgrimages that were imposed to make atonement for sins,
the distance might sometimes be proportional to the crime. For his part
in the murder of Walter Stapleton, the bishop of Exeter, in 1326, John
Laurence was compelled to go to Santiago de Compostela in north-west

Spain, and to visit on the way the shrines of the Virgin Mary at Boulogne and Le Puy, and that of Thomas Becket at Canterbury. The relationship between penance and pilgrimage in the Latin West had become tighter since the twelfth century, when papal indulgences were increasingly attached to specific destinations at specific times. Pope Boniface VIII responded to popular excitement about the centenary year 1300 by granting a plenary indulgence for pilgrims to the basilicas of the apostles in Rome. By observing the conditions of the indulgence, pilgrims would receive the total remission of all sins. The Florentine chronicler Giovanni Villani (d. 1348) describes how the Sudario, the cloth used by Veronica to wipe Christ's face at the carrying of the Cross and thereafter impressed with an image of Christ, was displayed in St Peter's at regular times throughout that year for the spiritual elevation of the pilgrims. He goes on to remark quite incidentally on the financial benefit of this:

Fig. 14
Pilgrim pendant
Italy, probably Rome, 15th century
Brass, D 3.4 cm

This pendant is embossed with a representation of the Sudario, the veil of St Veronica, miraculously impressed with an image of Christ's face.

The British Museum, London

> And it was the most remarkable thing that was ever seen, that during the whole year there were in Rome, besides the Roman people, 200,000 pilgrims, not counting those who were coming and going along the roads ... And from the offerings made by the pilgrims great treasures accrued to the church and to the Romans; all were made rich by their takings.[6]

St James – the pilgrims' saint
Rome, rich in the bodies of the martyrs and in possession of the relics of the apostles Peter and Paul, ranked highest among the places of penitential pilgrimage in Western Europe. It was followed by Santiago

Fig. 15
Pilgrim badge
Rome, dated 1500
Silver, W 5.5 cm

The relic of the Sudario is held on this badge by St Peter and St Paul, Rome's most significant saints.

The British Museum, London

de Compostela, with Cologne and Canterbury vying for third position. Santiago de Compostela relied for its success on the legend that the remains of the apostle St James were buried there. From the time of the discovery of his tomb in the early ninth century, pilgrims were attracted to his shrine in ever-increasing numbers. The cult of St James evolved against the constant threat of Muslim incursions into Christian Spain. According to the *General Chronicle* of Alfonso X of Castile (*c.* 1264), Ramiro I of Asturias (reigned 842–50) faced Muslim forces at Clavijo in 844. Vastly outnumbered, the Christians achieved victory only with the miraculous intervention of St James, who appeared with banner and sword, riding a white horse. It is not entirely certain that the battle actually occurred, but its story secured St James's reputation as a defender of Christian Spain. A fine fifteenth-century print from the workshop of Martin Schongauer demonstrates the continuing relevance of this conflict between Christians and Muslims throughout the medieval period [fig. 16]. In the print St James appears not as a military saint armed for battle, but essentially as a pilgrim on horseback, brandishing a sword.

The phenomenal appeal to pilgrims of Santiago de Compostela created the iconography of Saint James. His attributes were a pilgrim's hat adorned with a scallop shell and a pilgrim's staff, as seen in any number of representations [fig. 17]. The origin of the scallop shell as a symbol for the saint is unknown, but it became the more or less universal identifier of a pilgrim in the Middle Ages. Pilgrims were expected to be recognizable, partly for the hospitality that might be extended to them on the road. Their dress had certain practical

Fig. 16
The Battle of Clavijo
Workshop of Martin Schongauer
Germany, 1470–95
Engraving on paper, 28.9 x 42.9 cm

The British Museum, London

considerations, consisting of a wide-brimmed hat, a satchel or pouch and a staff [fig. 18]. Payment for pilgrim staffs was among the gifts made by the Opera di San Jacopo (the office of works) in Pistoia, Italy, which provided support for the expenses of poor pilgrims. Between about 1360 and 1480, the Opera dispensed payments to around three thousand pilgrims, the majority of whom were travelling to Santiago de Compostela. Pistoia had a special relationship with St James: in about 1140 a relic of the apostle arrived there through the negotiations between Bishop Atto and Rainerius, a Pistoian cleric resident at Santiago de Compostela. By 1145 an altar to St James was established and miracles attributed to the apostle had attracted the attention of the

Uu̇ser pilgerschaft sóll wir volbꝛingn mit gaiſtlichn fꝛödeṅ / in dem lob
gots vṅ in haltuṅg ſeiner gebot. Als Dauid ſpꝛicht. Cantabiles michi erãt
iuſtificãtõts tue / in loco peregrinationis mee. Hɇꝛ / deine gebot hab ich ge
ſuṅgṅ / in der zeit meiner pilgerſchaft. Wólche pilgerſchaft die kirch begeꝛt
võ dem erſten ſoṅtag ńach trinitatis / vṅtz zum erſten ſoṅtag des adueṅts.

Fig. 17
St James
Anonymous
Germany, c. 1480
Woodcut, 5.2 x 3.4 cm

The British Museum, London

Fig. 18
Pilgrims Passing a Wayside Shrine
Hans Burgkmair the Elder
Augsburg, Germany, c. 1510
Woodcut, 22.4 x 15.6 cm (sheet)

The British Museum, London

papacy. One of the early beneficiaries of the intercession of St James
at Pistoia was a man from San Baronto who was unable to walk due
to a muscular ailment. Once cured he immediately embarked upon a
pilgrimage to Santiago de Compostela to give thanks. This type of
spiritual contract was not unusual for pilgrims, who frequently
travelled to a particular shrine as a consequence of a promise made.
A dispensation granted by Pope John XXII (reigned 1316–34) in 1331
for a vow to make a pilgrimage reveals something of the mechanism
behind such commitments. It concerns Marguerite de Barri, whose
husband had vowed that if she were cured of a grave illness they would
both go on pilgrimage to Santiago de Compostela. Marguerite, though

cured, remained too frail to travel because of the effect of multiple childbirths (about twenty) and her advancing age. The vow was, therefore, converted into other pious works.

St Foy – saint or idol?

Santiago de Compostela drew pilgrims from every corner of Christendom and was instrumental in creating prosperity for other shrines that were on the major routes leading to it. John Laurence's pilgrimage, cited above, which was to take in Canterbury, Boulogne and Le Puy, was typical of the itinerary that an English pilgrim might make. Conques in the Auvergne could conceivably have served as an additional stopping point for Laurence as it did for others, attracted by the miracle-working image of St Foy [fig. 19]. The statue of St Foy contained relics of the saint, who was thought to have been martyred under Emperor Diocletian in 303. Her gem-encrusted golden appearance was intended to reflect her celestial state, but the three-dimensional modelling of the figure was troubling for some. Bernard of Angers, who compiled two books of the miracles of St Foy in the early years of the eleventh century, had first to overcome his initial feelings of unease for the effigy, which he describes as 'an image made with such precision to the face of the human form that it seemed to see with its attentive, observant gaze ...'.[7]

34

Bernard, however, felt that it was completely irrational to address prayers to 'a mute, insensate thing'.[8] A similar statue of St Gerald d'Aurillac had drawn from him a comparison with the pagan idols of Jupiter or Mars, and it was only exposure to accounts of St Foy's miracles that helped to dispel his fears. He concluded that

> Sainte Foy's image ought not to be destroyed or criticised, for it seems that no-one lapses into pagan errors because of it, nor does it seem that the powers of the saints are lessened by it, nor indeed does it seem that any aspect of religion suffers because of it.[9]

Statue reliquaries such as that of St Foy had first been conceived in the ninth century and were identified by Bernard as a regional speciality of the Massif Central. Their power of direct communication, as demonstrated by the gaze of St Foy in the passage quoted above, was exploited by the later development elsewhere of body-part or 'speaking reliquaries' (see p. 93).

Cologne – a second Rome

One of the most spectacular shrines to survive from the Middle Ages is that of the three Magi at Cologne [fig. 20], created over a number of years from about 1170 to 1230 by several different craftsmen, including the celebrated goldsmith Nicholas of Verdun (1130–1205). The most conventional form for the shrine of a saint was architectural. Derived from the ancient classical practice of enshrining remains in cinerary urns or sarcophagi influenced by temple design, the 'house-shaped' shrine became the customary repository for the bodies of the saints. Its point of reference was duly Christianized so that it represented not a pagan temple but the house of God. Its structure, therefore, was suitably lavish, taking its inspiration from biblical accounts of the heavenly Jerusalem: 'And the building of the wall of it was of jasper, and the city was pure gold, like unto clear glass' (Revelations 21:18). The shrine of the Magi consists of three consolidated, house-shaped units; two are arranged side by side and they are surmounted by a third to make a unified whole. The splendid decoration applied to every surface of the shrine includes filigree and enamel work, with a multitude of different gems and cameos. Along its walls vigorously rendered figures of apostles and prophets are arranged beneath arches, while at the front the Adoration of the Magi and the Baptism of Christ are set out beneath a representation of Christ enthroned. The relics of the three Magi – the kings from the east who followed a star leading them to place of Christ's birth – were allegedly discovered by the intrepid Empress Helena. Helena deposited the relics in Hagia Sophia in Constantinople, but c. 344 they were taken to Milan by Bishop Eustorgius (d. c. 350). Thereafter, they were removed from Milan to Cologne by the Holy Roman Emperor, Frederick Barbarossa (1122–90), in 1164. For Barbarossa, as

Fig. 20
The shrine of the Magi
Nicholas of Verdun and others
Germany, c. 1170–1230
Silver gilt, enamel and gems
over wooden core
153 x 220 x 110 cm

Cologne Cathedral

for Constantine before him, relics signified prestige, political might, physical protection and spiritual security. Cologne's importance as a pilgrimage destination, however, was based on a much longer list of saints' relics that could be found in the city. Pope Boniface IX (1356–1404) recognized the sheer density of saints represented there when he granted Cologne a jubilee indulgence in 1394

> ... by the virtues and merits of the Three Kings, who in the flesh offered three gifts to Christ the King ... of the most holy eleven thousand virgins; of the holy Thebans Gereon and his companions ... of the archbishop St Severinus ... and saints Cunibert, Ewald, Felix and Nabor, Gregory of Spoleto, Hippolitus, Felix and Audactus, Vitalis, Albinus and many other martyrs and confessors whose bodies and relics similarly repose in various monasteries and churches in the same place.[10]

Canterbury – murder in the cathedral

Work had probably barely begun on the shrine of the Magi in 1170 when the shocking news broke of the murder of Thomas Becket, archbishop of Canterbury (1118–70). Becket's martyrdom was largely to a political cause as he struggled to defend the rights and privileges of the Church against Henry II (1133–89). After a six-year period of exile, Becket returned to England in December 1170. By the end of that same month he had been brutally murdered in the nave of Canterbury Cathedral by four of Henry's knights. From the moment of his death, Becket was regarded spontaneously as a saint, and miracles were reported

Fig. 21
Life of St Thomas Becket
John of Salisbury
England, *c.* 1180
Parchment, 14 x 13 cm (picture)

The British Library, London

immediately at the site of the crime. After his canonization in 1173, Canterbury became the most prominent pilgrimage destination in England and ranked alongside Cologne as equal third in importance in Western Europe.

John of Salisbury (1115/20–80), who had served as Becket's secretary, collected his correspondence and gathered accounts of his miracles to compile a biography [fig. 21]. An illustration of the martyrdom is placed before John's account of the event and shows Becket being told of the arrival of the knights in the top register and his death at the point of a sword in the lower. This last scene is conflated with one that depicts the penance of the knights at Becket's tomb, which they approach as pilgrims, anxious to be as close as possible to the body of the saint. In a general note by John, the phenomenal miracles that he records resemble those performed by Christ in the Gospel, including the cure of the paralysed, the blind, the deaf, the lame, the healing of lepers and the raising of the dead.

Many of the reported cures were affected by the application of 'Canterbury water'. This miraculous draught consisted of Becket's blood diluted in holy water which was dispensed in small flasks made from a lead-tin alloy cast in moulds. One outstanding example [fig. 22] has on its front a high-relief figure of Becket between two of his assailants, while on the reverse is a depiction of his martyrdom framed by a border containing the phrase 'Optimus egrorum medicus fit Thoma bonorum' ('Thomas is the best doctor of the worthy sick'). This at once makes explicit Becket's great skill as a healer, but places the onus of a successful cure on the spiritual worthiness of the patient.

ne iusticia sua. humilis(que) & p(ro)mpta

modamine cuertav. Explicit ep(isto)la
q(uo) oct(ogesi)ma. Incipit octogesima p(r)ima.

1·11

below and opposite
Fig. 22
Pilgrim flask
Canterbury, *c.* 1170–1200
Lead-tin alloy, 10 x 8.7 cm

The reverse of the flask (below) is engraved
with the figure of Becket kneeling in prayer as
an assailant strikes him from behind with a
sword. On the front (opposite) Becket stands
between two armed knights.

The British Museum, London

The flasks for Canterbury water were only one of a very great
variety of cheaply manufactured mass-produced souvenirs for sale at
Canterbury. Some appear to have been designed deliberately to coincide
with significant events. A badge with the design of
Becket's shrine may have been made to
commemorate the translation of his body from
the crypt to a splendid new shrine at the east
end of the cathedral in 1220. Another
high-quality piece may have been cast
in or around 1320 to celebrate Becket's
third jubilee [fig. 23]. It takes the form
of a devotional plaque with a bust of
Becket and is one of the most numerous
in type to survive. Each piece has
sufficient detail in common to suggest
that their design may be based on the
reliquary bust of Becket that was
housed in the Corona Chapel. In
1314 Henry of Eastry, the cathedral's
prior, enriched the reliquary with
gold, silver and precious stones,
undoubtedly exciting both the
devotion and the donations of
pilgrims.

Becket's cult achieved international
fame through the sensational nature of his

40

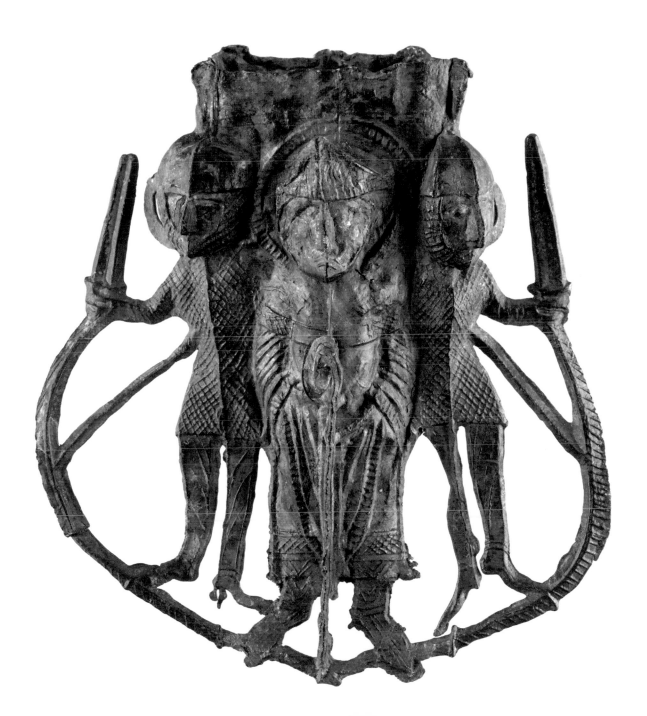

death. It was, however, also propagated abroad by the circulation of his relics and the patronage of the Plantagenets. Evidence suggests that when the daughters of Henry II married, Joanna to William the Good of Sicily and Eleanor to Alfonso VIII of Castile, they took relics of Becket with them, generating interest in the Canterbury saint in both Sicily and Spain (see p. 98). John of Salisbury did likewise when he became bishop of Chartres in 1176 and miracles attributed to the intercession of Becket were soon reported there. The presence of saints was seen as intrinsically mobile: they could exist in heaven with Christ and yet be located in several places on earth according to the distribution of their physical remains. Relics lost none of their power through dispersal and served as one of the most significant means of defining sacred space throughout the Middle Ages.

MATERIAL SPIRIT 2

COLLECTING RELICS

Fig. 24
View of Venice
from Bernhard von Breydenbach's
Travels to the Holy Land
Mainz, Germany, 1486
27.5 x 12.9 cm

The townscape of Venice as represented
here is still recognizable today. The main
embarkation point for pilgrims to the Holy
Land and crusaders was from the wharf
outside the Doge's palace.

The British Museum, London

VENICE WAS THE MAJOR POINT of departure for sea-faring pilgrims to the Holy Land from the West [fig. 24]. Longstanding historic, cultural and commercial links with the East ensured that it retained a multicultural atmosphere, but its strategic position also gave it certain military advantages. Venice figured strongly in the periodic crusades that were launched against Muslim control of the Holy Land throughout the Middle Ages. The most notorious, guided by the Venetians, was the Fourth Crusade, which ended in the Sack of Constantinople in 1204, when the crusaders directed their might against their Christian allies. Later attempts to justify the attack did little to eliminate the suspicion that the city was just too rich to resist.

The treasures of Constantinople

In terms of precious relics, Constantinople had no equal. The French knight, Robert de Clari, writing between about 1205 and 1215, described what he witnessed there:

> Within this chapel were found many rich relics: ... two pieces of the True Cross as large as the leg of a man ... and the iron of the lance with which Our Lord had his side pierced, and two of the nails which were driven through his hands and feet; and ... in a crystal phial quite a little of his blood and ... the tunic which he wore ... when they led him to Mount Calvary. And one found there also the blessed crown with which he was crowned ... and the robe of Our Lady....[11]

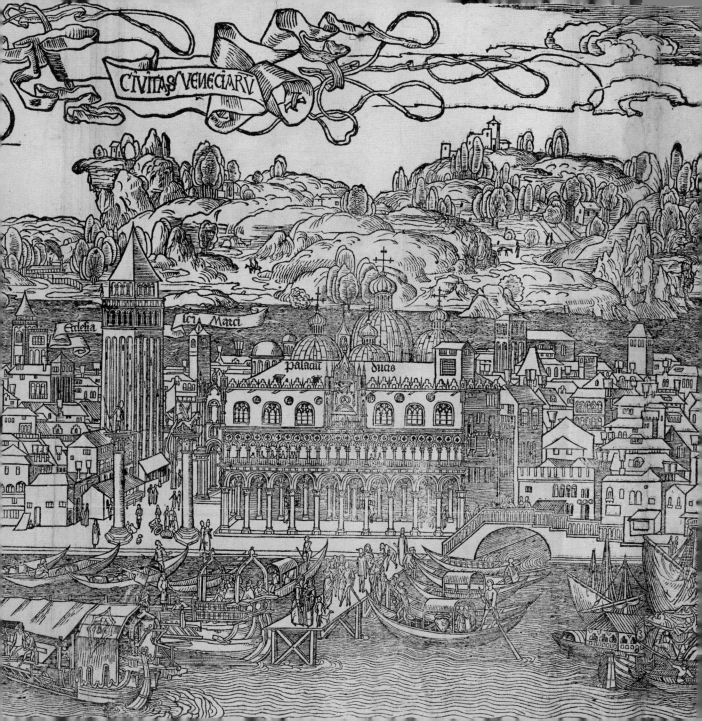

CIVITAS VENECIARV

Ecclesia   ſca Marci

palaciu   ducis

Fig. 25
Arm reliquary of St George
Venice, early 14th century with
16th-century additions
Exterior: silver gilt, enamels, glass
Interior: silver
Exterior H 51.9 cm, interior H 31 cm

The silver sheath shown on the right
originated in Constantinople (present-day
Istanbul) and was taken to Venice
after the Fourth Crusade in 1204.

Basilica di San Marco, Venice

Robert is referring to the contents of the imperial chapel of the Virgin of the Lighthouse, the Pharos, probably the most sacred Christian collection anywhere in the world at the time. Other relics held there included the arm of John the Baptist, the tablets of the law given to Moses on Mount Sinai, and the Mandylion, or holy towel, which bore a miraculous imprint of Christ's features.

A significant number of important relics were taken from Constantinople at the time of the Fourth Crusade, transforming the devotional landscape of Western Europe as they were widely disseminated. One of the principal personalities of this crusade, Doge Enrico Dandolo (d. 1205), sent to the church of San Marco in Venice a miracle-working cross that the Emperor Constantine had worn in battle, a pilgrim flask containing the Holy Blood, a piece of the skull of St John the Baptist and the arm of St George [fig. 25]. The latter arrived in Venice in a simple silver sheath engraved with a Greek inscription which translates 'Bearing the relic of St George the warrior; faith, fully armed, puts the enemy to flight', implying that the relic may have been borne on to the battlefield. Later, in the fourteenth century, the arm and its sheath were set into a more splendid reliquary decorated with foliate scrolls and translucent enamels.

Louis IX and Henry III – rival collectors

The vast sacred treasure houses that had been assembled by the Byzantine emperors heavily influenced the relic-gathering activities of Western monarchs, who put great store in both the volume and quality of their collections. Foremost among these royal collectors

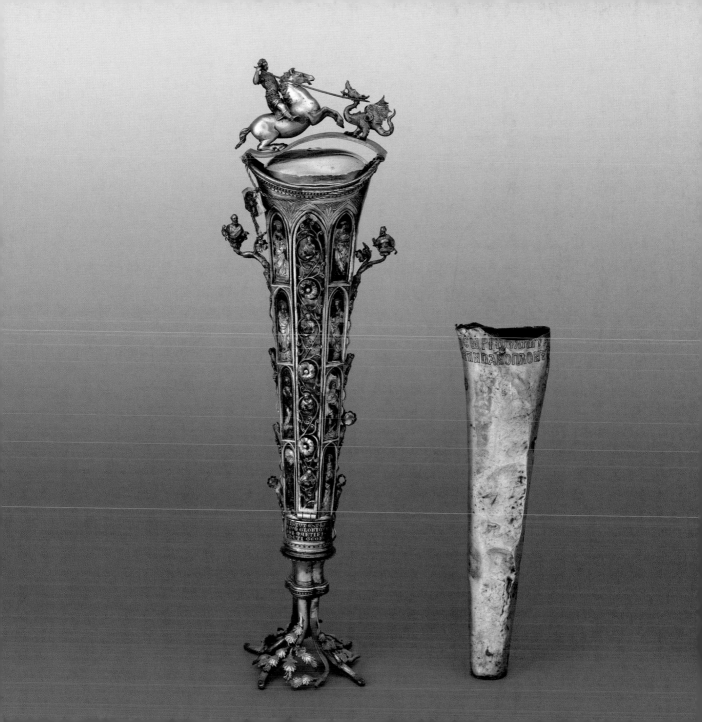

Fig. 26
Sainte Chapelle
Paris, consecrated 1248

was Louis IX of France (1214–70), who was able to benefit from the political changes that followed the Fourth Crusade. His cousin, the Latin emperor of Constantinople, Baldwin II (1217–73), was in permanent financial difficulty, faced with the demands of defending his enfeebled kingdom. In 1237 Baldwin pledged to Louis the Crown of Thorns that had been kept in the Pharos. When Louis arranged its transit to Paris the following year he was to discover that Baldwin had pawned the relic to a Venetian bank. Finally, however, in 1239 the Crown of Thorns was received by Louis at the staggering cost of 135,000 livres – a sum that constituted half the annual expenditure of the realm and one proportionately far greater than any modern-day defence budget. His investment in the spiritual welfare of the kingdom did not stop there. Following the precedent set by the imperial palace in Constantinople, Louis began building a royal chapel as a suitable repository for his wonderful acquisition. The mesmerizing Sainte Chapelle in Paris was the outcome [fig. 26]. This soaring, quintessentially gothic structure appears to defy gravity as if supported by walls of stained glass. It was conceived as a giant reliquary and by the time of its consecration in 1248 it was equipped with a total of twenty-two splendid relics obtained from Constantinople. The judgement made at the reception of the Crown of Thorns in 1239 by Gauthier Cornut, archbishop of Sens, that France had succeeded the Holy Land for the veneration of the Passion was now truer than ever.

Louis IX's collecting interests found close competition from Henry III of England (1207–72), who actively sought to endow Westminster Abbey with relics equal to those obtained by the French king. Henry,

Fig. 27
Henry III carries the relic of the Holy
Blood to Westminster Abbey
From *Chronica majora*
Matthew Paris
England, 1253–9
Parchment, 35.8 x 24.4 cm (folio)

The Parker Library, Corpus Christi College,
Cambridge

too, sourced items from the Holy Land, using his connections with
the Knights Hospitaller, a military order charged with the care and
protection of pilgrims who journeyed there. Between 1234 and 1235
Henry received, among others, relics of the Golden Gate of Jerusalem,
the Holy Sepulchre, Calvary, the altar of the Presentation of Christ
and – most extraordinary of all – a relic of the Burning Bush.
Henry's equivalent prestige relic to the Crown of Thorns was a
relic of the Holy Blood. The blood spilt by Christ at the time of
the Crucifixion – the most emotive and compelling evidence of
his sacrifice – was considered by many to be more worthy than
the Crown of Thorns, which had been sanctified only by contact
with the blood. Henry had negotiated the gift from the Patriarch
of Jerusalem, who was petitioning him with requests to mount a
crusade. The relic was received at Westminster with due pomp and
ceremony in 1247, neatly timed before Louis IX's consecration of
Sainte Chapelle. The occasion was commemorated at Henry's
invitation in Matthew Paris's *Chronica majora* [fig. 27]. The
manuscript shows Henry carrying the relic of the Holy Blood in
a crystal container in solemn procession from St Paul's Cathedral
to Westminster Abbey. Oddly, the Westminster relic was never to
achieve the same glory as the Crown of Thorns in Paris. It failed
to motivate pilgrims, who seem to have regarded it with some
suspicion, preferring the relic of the Holy Blood at Hailes Abbey.
This is an interesting reflection on the discernment of pilgrims
who clearly made judgements about the quality and origins of
the relics they favoured.

gaudium. et qui non orat pro se et facit pro ea sua immo
nummos et universalis esse orare, immo rapinis inhiat
pecunie indefessus. dicimusque et est affirmatum, quod non
sub lachrimis scribi debet vel cum singultibus recitari. plus con-
fidit in pecunie thesauris quam fidelium precibus vel
elemosinis. Magnates Alemannie elegerunt

In crastino vero Willelmum comitem Hollandie in festo sancti Michaelis magnates regem suum et ei homagium tes Alemannie ad quos ius electionis ligium fecerunt tionis spectat pro maiori parte: elegerunt sibi ultimo in regem alemannie Willelmum comitem hollandie adolescentem. habentem in etate circiter xx. annos. iuvenem elegantem et probum atque genere suo. Cui et fecerunt homagium. Dux tamen saxonie et quidam alii magnates huic electioni non consenserunt. Unde magister quidam surrepsit in hec dicens. Ecce militia que sacerdocium per superbia. Ecce sacerdocium eadem cum qua militia.

Circa idem tempus scripsit dominus rex De sanguine omnibus regni sui magnatibus Christi allato Lond. ut in festo sancti Edwardi videlicet translatione que celebratur in quindena sancti Michaelis: iubens ut omnes ibidem convenirent: ut iocundissimos eidem sancti beneficium celitus anglis nuper collati gauderet et postea ut tam gloriosi regis et martyris translationem venerarentur. Tercio: ut Willelmi de valentia fratris sui uterini quem ipse rex ea die baltheo cincturus

cum summo honore et reverentia ac timore accipiens illud vasculum cum thesauro memorato: tulit illud ferens in propatulo super faciem suam. iens pedes. habens humilem habitum. scilicet pauperem capam sine capucio precedentibus vestitis prodiit sine pausatione. usque ad ecclesiam Westmonasterii. que distat ab ecclesia sancti pauli circiter uno miliari. Nec pretermittendum. quod ambabus manibus illud deferens: cum per stratam salebrosam et inequalem pergeret: semper vel in celum vel in ipsum vas lumina tenebat defixa. Supportabatur autem palla per iiii. hastas. Supportabantque duo coadiutores brachia sua ne in tanto forte labore deficeret.

Conventus autem Westmonasterii cum omnibus qui convenerant episcopis abbatibus et monachis qui plus quam centum estimabantur. canentes et exultantes in spiritu sancto et lacrimis: occurrebant eidem domino regi sic advenienti usque ad portam curie episcopi dunelmensis. Tunc autem reversi sicut venerat videlicet processionaliter ad ecclesiam Westmonasterii: ubi in ea per copiosa turbe multitudine continebantur. Nec adhuc cessabat dominus rex quin indefessus ferens illud vas ut prius circuire ecclesiam. Regiam et thalamos suos. Demum illud quasi donum inpreciabile quod totam angliam ditando illustraverat: donavit et optulit deo et ecclesie sancti petri Westmonasterii et caro suo Edwardo. et sacro conventui qui ibidem deo et sanctis suis ministrant.

Sequelatur conventus Westmonasterii cum abbatibus et monachis quos longum esset enumerare festive vestitis et canentibus et classico magno pulsato

Relics of the Crown of Thorns

The relic of the Crown of Thorns continued to maintain a high profile in French devotional culture. What remains of the relic today is encased in a reliquary dating from the Napoleonic period in the cathedral of Notre Dame, Paris. It lacks even a solitary thorn, and is probably a shadow of the object that Louis acquired in 1239. We have little precise information about its appearance at that time, although the practice of the Byzantine emperors of breaking off thorns as diplomatic gifts was continued by the French kings and may account for its present thornless appearance. The custom is illustrated in a print dating from about 1490, which shows Louis presenting a single thorn to the bishop of Vicenza, Bartolomeo da Breganze, in 1259 [fig. 28]. In 1260 Bartolomeo founded the Church of the Holy Crown in honour of the precious relic. The print may have been designed to commemorate the completion of the crypt in 1482 that was to accommodate the thorn.

Two thorns preserved in the British Museum are contained in reliquaries with medieval French royal provenances and are thus likely to originate from Louis' Crown of Thorns. The first is an intensely private jewel that reveals its sacred content gradually through symbol and image [fig. 29]. When closed it resembles the large pendant gems popular in secular society around the mid-fourteenth century. It consists of a cover of brilliant amethyst set into gold mounts forming a hinged locket which is secured shut by pins. The amethyst, impressive in both size and quality, is given extra lustre by a backing of silver foils. When open its intricacy is entrancing. It unfolds rather like a miniature book, with surfaces rendered in the most vibrant translucent enamels.

Fig. 29
The Holy Thorn pendant
Paris, c. 1340
Gold, enamel, amethyst, glass, rock crystal, parchment
4 x 2.65 x 2.5 cm

The first leaf includes a donor portrait in the fashion of a manuscript illumination, depicting a king and his queen in adoration of the Virgin and Child. The scenes opposite show the Flight into Egypt (bottom) and the Presentation in the Temple (top), using a narrative order running from top to bottom, the convention for reading stained glass panels. The second part of the jewel contains, on the left side, a scene of the Nativity placed above the Annunciation to the shepherds. This panel is distinctive because it consists of a piece of painted parchment placed beneath a layer of modern glass. It conceals a secret chamber at the heart of the pendant that contains the relic of the Holy Thorn set into a central compartment. The relic is sealed by a crystal cover and set beneath a gold crown. Other compartments surrounding the thorn may once have contained additional relics. On the left a plaque carries an inscription in alternate letters of red and blue: 'De Spina: Sancte: Corone' ('Of the thorn of the Holy Crown'). In its exposed state, the thorn appears opposite a representation of the Crucifixion (bottom) and the Deposition from the Cross (top), maintaining the upside-down order of the scenes. Intriguingly, the Crown of Thorns is not worn by Christ in these depictions – presumably because it is evoked through the thorn that is actually embedded in the jewel.

The British Museum, London

Fig. 30
The Holy Thorn reliquary
Paris, 1390–97
Gold, enamel, rock crystal,
pearls, rubies, sapphires
H 30.5 cm

The front and back of the
Holy Thorn reliquary.

The British Museum, London

The style and technical details of the reliquary suggest that it is the work of a Parisian goldsmith dating from about 1340. Given this, it is most likely that the royal couple portrayed inside the pendant are Philippe VI (1293–1350) and his queen Jeanne de Bourgogne. Philippe appears barefoot, probably in imitation of St Louis who left Paris for the Seventh Crusade in the same manner.

The British Museum's second relic of the Holy Thorn is displayed in a much more theatrical setting [figs 30 and 31]. The Holy Thorn reliquary from the Waddesdon Bequest is a tour de force of Parisian goldsmiths' work, dated by the heraldic plaques inserted into its castellated base to between about 1390 and 1397. The heraldry relates to the French prince, Jean duc de Berry, the brother of Charles V (1338–80), who commissioned the piece. In a central compartment, behind a vitrine of rock crystal, mounted on a monstrously large sapphire, is a thorn of equally grand proportions. The thorn appears at the centre of a Last Judgement scene inhabited by three-dimensional figures in gold, enlivened by the application of enamels, rubies and pearls. Christ, seated on a rainbow with a globe at his feet, displays his wounds, while angels encircle his head bearing the instruments of the Passion. Beneath Christ, to either side, the Virgin Mary and John the Baptist kneel in prayer. This scene is framed by a dynamic arrangement of the twelve apostles with a figure of God the Father in heaven at the top. The base forms the terrestrial sphere, shown as a grassy mound dotted with open graves yielding the bodies of the resurrected dead, while angels sound the last trump. On the reverse the themes of death and judgement are developed on two gold doors that enclose

a compartment for a second relic (now missing). On the left, executed
in low relief, is a figure of St Michael who appears in Last Judgement
scenes weighing the souls of the dead; and on the right, St Christopher,
who protected against sudden death. The reliquary is forceful, energetic
and loaded with drama. However, although the crowded composition
almost obscures the relic, the thorn is essentially always visible and acts
as the permanent focus for veneration.

The Crown of Thorns had a very particular relevance for the French
monarchy. Symbolically it signified the one true king who would return
in judgement at the Second Coming. The antiphon composed for the
formal reception of the relic at Sens in 1239 described it as being sent
by the supreme king to the king of France. It goes on to view the Crown
of Thorns as a sacred deposit on loan until Christ came to claim it back
on the Day of Judgement, when the realm of France would become
the kingdom of heaven. It was surely this belief that informed Louis'
collection, and the same conviction that determined the subject matter
of the Waddesdon Bequest Holy Thorn reliquary.

Charles IV and the Holy Roman Empire

Louis IX's impact on the monarchical ideal was considerable –
particularly after his canonization in 1297. France now had its dynastic
saint and other rulers looked to him as an exemplar of the Christian
king. This is especially apparent in the case of the Holy Roman Emperor
Charles IV (1316–78). Charles was educated in Paris at the Capetian
court, where he experienced the ritual surrounding the royal veneration
of the Passion relics at Sainte Chapelle. In the 1340s he began the

Fig. 32
Reliquary pendant
England, late 15th century
Gold, enamel
5 x 4.2 cm

This gold and enamel reliquary pendant
would have been owned by a person
of some wealth. The wearing of relics
in personal jewels was a feature of late
medieval piety; numerous wills and
inventories of the late fourteenth and
fifteenth century testify to the practice.
The figure of St John the Baptist is
engraved on the front of the reliquary
above a French inscription that has
been interpreted as meaning 'At my
death'. The bishop saint on the reverse
is probably St Thomas Becket. Around
the edges of the reliquary, tears are
engraved which may suggest that
this was a mourning jewel.

The British Museum, London

Fig. 33
The Chapel of the Holy Cross
1348–57
Karlstejn Castle, near Prague

process of furnishing his palace chapel with relics and the activity accelerated with his election as Holy Roman Emperor in 1346. In 1350 the imperial relics and insignia arrived in Prague where they were publicly displayed. Charles built Karlstejn Castle close to Prague as a permanent home for them, creating the Chapel of the Holy Cross which rivalled Sainte Chapelle in its lavish decoration [fig. 33]. It, too, resembled a giant reliquary. Its vaults were covered in gilded stucco set with glass gems, and its walls were studded with polished agate, amethyst, jasper and carnelian in an attempt to evoke the heavenly Jerusalem (see p. 36).

In 1424 Charles' son, Emperor Sigismund (1368–1437), transferred the imperial treasures to Nuremberg for safekeeping during the Hussite Wars. There they were popularized in print in 1480 and then again in 1496 [fig. 34]. Printed sheets with images of relics from specific shrines or churches were known as *Heiltumsblätter*. On one level they served as souvenirs and on another as advertisements for the treasures that pilgrims might expect to encounter on their travels, but they also acted as affordable aids to devotion. Of the relics that could be contemplated on the sheet from

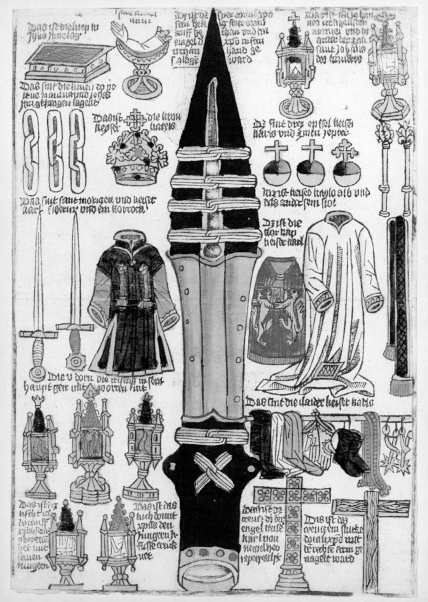

Nuremberg are the sword, robe and sceptre of Charlemagne – ancient
regalia of the Holy Roman Empire that had achieved the status of relic.
Central to the composition is an oversized representation of the spear
believed to have pierced the side of Christ at the Crucifixion. This was
apparently drawn to scale to encourage a more vivid visualization of
the event.

Frederick the Wise's relic collection at Wittenberg

More extensive publications of relic collections were compiled as books
for sale to pilgrims. Known as a Heiltumsbuch, or relic book, it consisted
of illustrations with captions of text itemizing multifarious relics with
occasional descriptions of the reliquaries that contained them. Relic
books were sold at the annual exposure of the relics to pilgrims, usually
a crowd-pulling event to which was attached the granting of indulgences
(see p. 30).

At Wittenberg in Saxony a phenomenally large collection of relics
brought with it cumulative indulgences of immense numbers of years.
The collection was accommodated in the Chapel of All Saints at the
castle of Wittenberg, which was founded by Rudolph I (1298–1356),
elector of Saxony, and used to house a relic of the Holy Thorn given to
him by Philippe VI of France (see pp. 56–8). When Frederick the Wise
(1463–1526) moved to Wittenberg he rebuilt the castle and began to
endow the chapel with ever-increasing quantities of relics so that his
collection grew from a very respectable 5,005 relics in 1509 to an
astounding 19,015 in 1520. The early collection was commemorated
by a relic book with illustrations by Lucas Cranach the Elder, printed

Dye zaigung des hochlobwirdigen hailigthums der Stifft kirchen aller hailigen zu wittenburg

Fig. 35
Relic book
Illustrated by Lucas Cranach the Elder
Wittenberg, 1510
Woodcut, 20.1 x 14.1 cm

This second edition detailing the relics
of Wittenberg contained 119 woodcuts
by Cranach.

The British Museum, London

in two editions in 1509 and 1510 [fig. 35]. Cranach was one of two celebrated artists who were patronized by Frederick. The second was Albrecht Dürer, who painted for him *The Martyrdom of the Ten Thousand Christians* (1508) for the relic chamber in Wittenberg. Dürer had also produced a woodcut of the same scene in 1496–7, which portrays the mythical torture and massacre of ten thousand Christians by the Persian king Saporat in the second century [fig. 36]. The event was of specific interest to Frederick because he held relics of these martyrs in his vast

Fig. 36
The Martyrdom of the
Ten Thousand Christians
Albrecht Dürer
Germany, 1496–7
Woodcut, 39.2 x 28.4 cm

The British Museum, London

aßlas in zaigung des hailigthumbs zu einem yeden gang hundert tag
Vnd von einem yeden stuck oder partickel desselben der vber etlich tau=
sent seint hundert tag aplas gebett Es mag ouch ein yeder mensch/ der
die Stifftkirchen besucht mit seine ynnigem gebet vnd von den altarien
ainem yeden ainen mercklichen aplas verdienen So ist ouch die vilbe=
melt kirchen mit dem aplas vergebung Peyn vnd schuld so zu Assias
da sant Franciscus leyblich rastet des ersten tags Augusti yn d Capeln
sant Marien de angelis Jerlich ist zwen tag vor vnd noch allerheilige
tag von dem Babst Bonifacio dem newnten gnedigklich begabt vnd
versehen Welcher aplas an wenige orten dan zu Assias vñ diser kirche
befunden Das allen frümen christen menschen zu besserung yres lebens
Vnd merung yrer seligkait. nit hat sollen verborgen sein noch bleiben
Vnd volgt die zaigung des hailigthumbs diser maß vnd gestalt.

Der erst gang Jn welchem angezaigt wirdt das wirdig hailigthumbs von Jungfrawen vnd Witwen

Erstlich wirt hie gezaigt

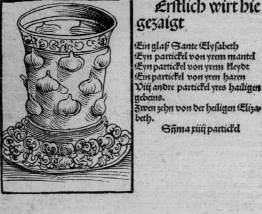

Ein glaß Sante Elysabeth
Eyn partickel von yrem mantel
Eyn partickel von yrem kleydt
Ein partickel von yren haren
Vili andre partickel yres hailigen gebeins.
Zwen zehen von der heiligen Eliza=
beth

Summa riiij partickel

left
Fig. 37
Hedwig beaker
Possibly Egypt or Syria, 12th century
Glass, H 14.3 cm

One of fourteen surviving glass beakers associated with the legend of St Hedwig.

The British Museum, London

Fig. 38
Page from the Wittenberg relic book
Illustrated by Lucas Cranach the Elder
Wittenberg, 1510
Woodcut, 20.1 x 14.1 cm

The page illustrates the Hedwig beaker owned by Frederick the Wise.

The British Museum, London

collection. They were displayed to the public each year on the second Sunday after Easter until 1523, when the changing religious climate inhibited Frederick's collecting impulse and compelled him to revert to a private ritual of annual veneration until his death in 1525. In a very real sense Frederick's collection became the victim of its conspicuousness, attracting the attention of another famous resident of Wittenberg, Martin Luther. The fantastic number of relics to be seen at the castle and the system of indulgences that accompanied pilgrimage there were undoubtedly instrumental in shaping Luther's reforming zeal that sought to overturn what he considered to be an abuse of the Church.

Of all of the relics that were amassed by Frederick the Wise, only one survives. It is a glass vessel that is one in a series of uncertain origin, possibly made in Egypt or Syria, known as the Hedwig beakers [fig. 37]. They date from the twelfth century and relate to the legend of St Hedwig (c. 1175–1243), whose abstention from drinking wine troubled her husband, until he witnessed the water in her glass transform miraculously into wine as she raised it to her lips. The beakers were thought to have belonged to Hedwig and were duly treasured as evidence of the miracle. The Hedwig beaker from Wittenberg appears to have survived because it clearly lacked bullion value when the rest of Frederick's sacred treasures were presumably

Fig. 39
The Andechs Chronicle

Bavaria, Germany, 1496
Woodcut, 26.5 x 75 cm

Beneath the neatly ordered rows of reliquaries is a depiction
of the bodies of the many saints held at the monastery.

The British Museum, London

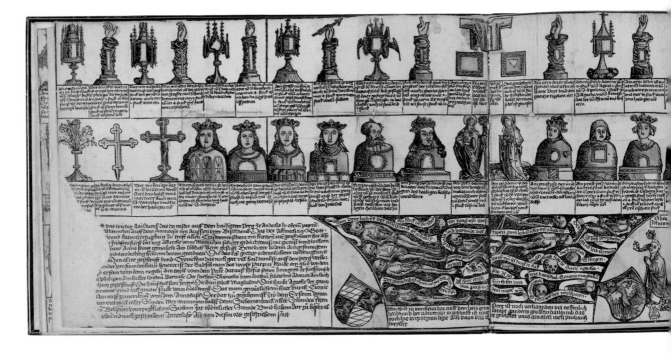

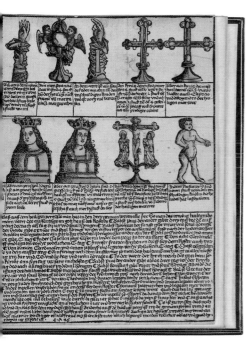

melted down. However, it seems that it was also preserved because it was allegedly given to Luther by Frederick's grandson, Johann Frederick (1503–54), thereby somewhat ironically becoming a secular relic of the great reformer.

The monastery of Andechs

St Hedwig was born at the castle of Andechs in Bavaria, the centre of another striking aristocratic relic collection that was to form the foundation of a Benedictine monastery church in 1455. The fame of the collection and its attraction for pilgrims had a much longer history, however, recorded in a printed chronicle published in five separate editions between about 1473 and 1500. This detailed the major relics to be seen, an abridged account of miracles that had occurred, and the monastery's connection with prominent nobles and clerics [figs 39 and 40]. To express it in very modern terms, the Andechs monastery benefited from developments in printing which helped to promote the strengths of its collection in a very competitive sector. Printing represented for the Middle Ages an information revolution with an impact as great as that of the internet today. From 1388 interest in Andechs was substantially heightened following the discovery of a marvellous cache of relics. The legend, as related in the chronicle, describes how a mouse deposited a vellum label on the altar during mass that had been tied around one of the relics and thus alerted the clergy to the whereabouts of the treasures. In fact, the relics had been hidden for safe-keeping as long ago as 1248 during a conflict with the House of Wittelsbach and their miraculous 'resurrection' caused an

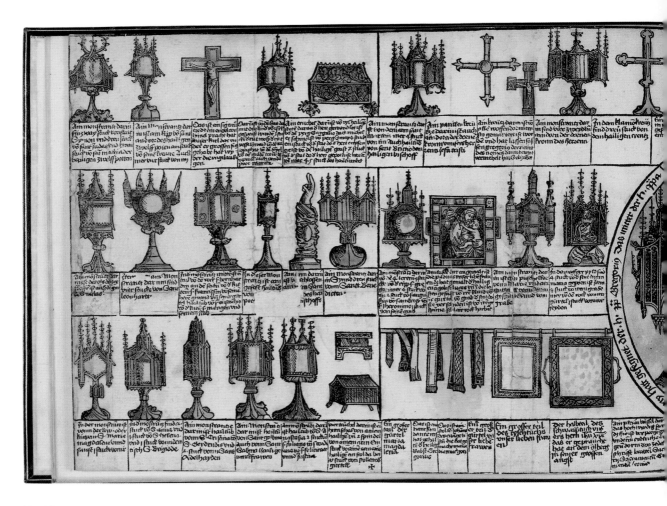

Fig. 40
The Andechs Chronicle
Bavaria, Germany, 1496
Woodcut, 26.5 x 75 cm

More than a hundred reliquaries are represented on the two broadsides
for the monastery at Andechs. The vast majority of them, as demonstrated
by this illustration, were purposefully designed to display their contents.

The British Museum, London

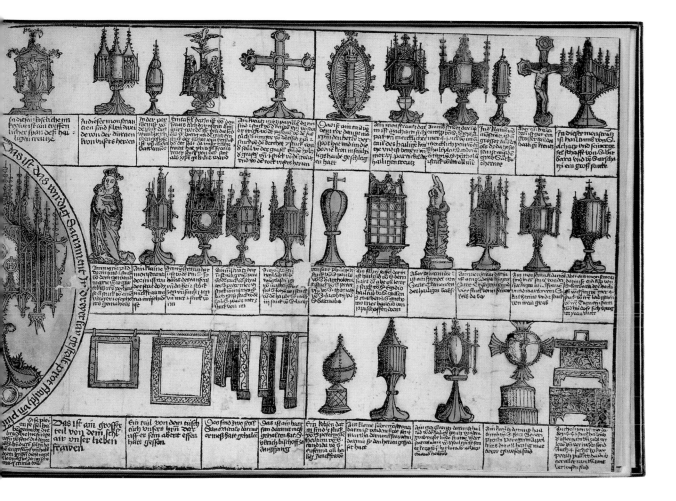

73

understandably significant stir. In 1455 Duke Albrecht III of Bavaria changed the status of the church at Andechs by endowing it as a monastic foundation complete with study, refectory, dormitories and seven Benedictine monks.

Basel and the St Eustace reliquary head

Monasteries and cathedral churches were frequently well stocked with prize relics contained in treasuries as rich as those of any emperor, king or prince. Influential friends, however, were vital to help construct and furnish the buildings with relics. The cathedral at Basel was rebuilt in 917, after the destruction caused by the Magyar raids, and consecrated in 1019. From this time onwards, the church began to accumulate sacred treasures, many of the earliest of which were gifts from the Holy Roman Emperor, Henry II (973–1024). The treasury survived the liturgical changes brought by the Protestant Reformation which the city embraced in 1529, only for half of it to be dispersed in the early nineteenth century as a consequence of civic reform. It was at this time that the British Museum's reliquary head of St Eustace found its way on to the open market, along with other pieces that were purchased by leading museums around the world. The St Eustace reliquary head [figs 41 and 42] has no iconography or inscription to substantiate that it was intended to contain relics of that legendary early Christian martyr. The earliest known description of it as the head of St Eustace comes from an inventory of 1477. When the reliquary was opened for conservation reasons in 1955, skull fragments were indeed found inside a cavity within its wooden core. Although they were unlabelled,

Fig. 41
Reliquary head of St Eustace
Switzerland, c. 1180–1200
Silver gilt, rock crystal, chalcedony,
amethyst, carnelian, pearl and glass
(wooden core with gesso [fig. 42])
35 x 16.6 x 18.4 cm

According to legend, St Eustace was a Roman general who converted to Christianity after a miraculous vision: when out hunting he saw a stag, which carried between its antlers an image of the crucified Christ. He and his family were later martyred for their faith. This head reliquary has been associated with the saint since 1477. It has two parts: a wooden core, which accommodated the relics, and a silver-gilt cover.

The British Museum, London

contrary to the usual practice whereby relics would
normally have vellum tags attached to them for
identification purposes (see p. 90), they may have
formed the original contents of the reliquary,
determining both its form and its name. These
were not the only relics sealed inside the head.
Others, neatly labelled and wrapped in colourful
textiles, included relics of St Eucharius, St
Nicholas of Myra, St Benedict, St Anastasius, St
Jocanda, and St Anthony, along with Passion relics of
the True Cross, the Holy Reed and a fragment of the
garment of Christ. The reliquary head's wooden core
was discovered at the same time. Made of sycamore, it
provided support for the metal sheets that later covered
it. Differences in modelling, however, and a surface
treatment suggesting that it may have been painted,
imply that the wooden head could have functioned
independently before the metal casing was fixed to it.
The silver-gilt sheets that covered the wooden head
were thought the most appropriate embellishment for
a reliquary, the purity of the precious metal carrying
with it certain symbolic values. Extra visual richness is
supplied to the reliquary by the application of filigree
and gems in a diadem that encircles the brow of the
saint. There are sixteen settings in all that contain
amethyst, carnelian, rock crystal, chalcedony, pearl

and glass. The pedestal on which the head stands was decorated
with gems on its top surface, although all but two are now lost.
The material structure of the St Eustace head – its wooden core,
silver-gilt plates and gem-encrusted diadem and the textiles that
were used to protect the relics placed inside it – illustrates the high
artistic values that were invested in reliquary manufacture. The finest
commodities and the most able craftsmen were employed to create
works that communicated something of the heavenly to those
fortunate enough to gaze upon them.

SACRED CRAFT 3

PATRONS, ARTISTS AND INDUSTRY

E VERY RELIQUARY YIELDS variable amounts of information about its commission, manufacture, ownership, dedication and use. The St Eustace reliquary head (see pp. 74–7) demonstrates that critical documentation concerning the identity of even the finest pieces can either be lost or omitted from records. Where other documentary evidence is lacking but the object carries an inscription, we can begin imaginatively at least to reconstruct something of its personal history.

A small enigmatic reliquary made to contain multiple relics, including one of the True Cross, suggests which shrine it was destined for through the saints listed in an inscription running around its edge [fig. 43]. The reliquary consists of a domed crystal cover over a bed of pearls sewn on to a gold plate with wire loops. In its centre is a simple wooden cross set into a gold surround, generally considered not to be a relic for two reasons. Firstly, it is a little early in the development of reliquary design for the relic to be displayed so boldly: there was an initial reluctance by the Church to make sacred relics visible that gradually diminished in the course of the thirteenth century. Secondly, and perhaps more significantly, a separate back-plate was fashioned by the goldsmith specifically to hold all the relics in place. Although now empty, a central compartment with a cross-shaped cavity was undoubtedly designed to contain the principal relic of the True Cross. This is surrounded by other cavities of different shapes made to hold an additional eleven relics. According to the inscription, the relics comprised one relating to Christ (the True Cross), one to St Ninian and others. Since St Ninian's name follows immediately after Christ's

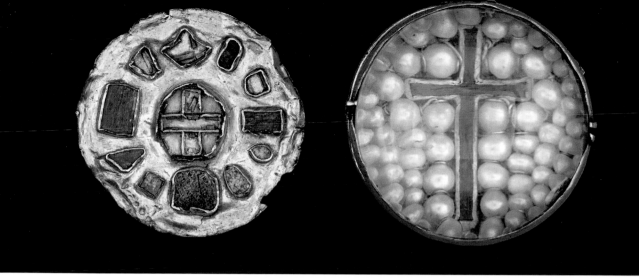

in the inscription, he is clearly a saint of significant interest within the reliquary's scheme. St Ninian was particularly venerated at the cathedral of Galloway at Whithorn in Scotland, and his relics are grouped here with other saints that have Scottish affiliations such as St Andrew, St Fergus, St Margaret and, more unusually, St Norbert. St Norbert of Xanten founded the Premonstratensian order of Canons Regular, under whose rule the cathedral of Galloway served. The magnificence of this opulent little jewel has led to the conviction that it was owned by a bishop of Galloway early in the thirteenth century, who may have worn it suspended around his neck or offered it to the shrine of St Ninian for the public veneration of visiting pilgrims.

Saints: patrons and protectors

Saints were invoked as specialists to intercede in areas considered appropriate to their life or martyrdom. They were accordingly made the patrons of professions and guilds. St Catherine, for instance, who was tortured on a wheel to compel her to relinquish Christ, became

below and opposite
Figs 44 and 45
Bell and bell shrine of St Conall Cael
Inishkeel, Ireland
Bell: 7th–9th century
Brass mount: *c.* 1000
Shrine: 15th century
Bell and mount: iron, copper alloy
Shrine: gilt bronze, silver, rock crystal
Bell and mount: 17 x 12.8 x 8.5 cm
Shrine: 21.9 x 15.5 x 12.7 cm

The bell (right) consists of a simple sheet
of iron that was embellished around 1000
with an inlaid brass plate. In the fifteenth
century, it was given an elaborate shrine
case (below) with figures of Christ and
the saints on the front, and engraved
images of the apostles on the reverse.

The British Museum, London

the patron saint of wheelwrights; St Apollonia, whose teeth were
wrenched out, was the patron of the barber surgeons who dealt with
dental problems in the Middle Ages. Specialism aside, most saints were
credited with the ability of affecting a wide variety of cures. The sixth-
century Irish bishop St Conall Cael's miraculous power was invoked
through a bell owned by him (figs 44 and 45). Water drunk from it
by pilgrims to St Conall's well on the island of Inishkeel was considered
to have miraculous healing power for any number of ailments.

For knights, the chivalric St George had particular appeal in both
the Byzantine East and Latin West. It may be this relationship that is
manifested in an intimate but elaborate jewel-like reliquary from
the British Museum's collection, which combines image and
inscription to provide evidence of its use and ownership
[fig. 46, overleaf]. Its front cover is missing, but on the reverse
is a representation of St George beautifully rendered in the
most delicate cloisonné enamels. The enamel is laid into
cells created by thin walls of gold wire and used to pick
out astonishing detail, particularly in the drapery. St
George directs his gaze to his sword, which rests on his
shoulder and points towards letters spelling out his name.
Another inscription in white letters on a brilliant blue
background encircles the central portrait medallion
with the words: '[The wearer] prays that you will be
his fiery defender in battles'. It is this inscription,
combined with the prominence of St George, that
establishes the military status of the owner.

Fig. 46
Pendant reliquary
Probably Thessalonike, 13th century
Gold, silver, silver gilt, enamel
D 3.8 cm

The reverse of the pendant is decorated with a figure of
St George (below). The front cover, though missing, would
have held a roundel of St Demetrios whose recumbent body
can be seen on an enamelled door inside the reliquary.
Within the compartment it encloses there is another
image of the saint lying on his tomb.

The British Museum, London

Fig. 47
Portable altar (reverse)
Hildesheim, Germany, *c*. 1200
Copper gilt over a wood core, limestone,
painted vellum, rock crystal, ivory
35.4 x 25.1 cm

The altar contains the relics of forty saints
whose names are inscribed on the reverse.

The British Museum, London

From a closely comparable pendant at Dumbarton Oaks, Washington, we can deduce what would have decorated the missing front cover. It combines the military saints Demetrios on the front, and Sergios and Bakchos on the reverse. Both pendants open to reveal a recumbent figure of a saint in a tomb. The inscriptions that accompany the Washington pendant make it clear that this figure is St Demetrios, whose shrine attracted pilgrims to Thessalonike eager to collect the sacred oil that oozed from his shrine. It is this substance that is alluded to in an inscription around the edge of the British Museum pendant, which states: 'Anointed by your blood and your myrrh'. A dark waxy residue can still be found in the spaces that surround the recumbent St Demetrios, but it is unclear whether this is the original relic or whether it relates to the pendant's later history. An eighteenth-century inscription engraved on the frame that has replaced the front cover explains that the pendant was once owned by the Georgian martyr Queen Kethevan, who used it to contain a relic of the True Cross.

A portable altar from Hildesheim

The continuous use of reliquaries that might be replenished with new relics or be replaced altogether by a new vessel explains something of the diversity of relics that are often found together. When relics for the portable altar from Hildesheim (figs 47–9) were assembled at the end of the twelfth century, it is likely that they came from a variety of sources, including existing reliquaries. In some cases, the textile wrappings that surround them are of a significantly earlier date than the altar itself. The relic of St Benedict, for instance, is wrapped in a

· IOҺIS · BAPT · PAVLI · APLI · IACOBII · P̃ · OAҺEI ·

· AP · Φ · EW · IOҺIS · EW · STEPҺANI · PT̃OO͂ · LAVRENTII ·

· VITI · CORNELII · CIPRIANI · FABIANI · SEBASTIANI · BONIFACII · EPI ·

· BLASII · EPI · FELICIS · CRISTOPҺORI · COSME · DAOIANI · PAN ·

· CPATIF · ҺEODORI · DIONISII · EPI · OARELLINI · PETRI ·

· CIPRIANI · IPOLITI · VITALIS · FELICISSIO · OAVRICII · ACINCTI · TOT ·

· NATEELICIS · NARORIS · O͂ RO͂ · ETCO͂ · CONFESSO͂ · GODEҺARDI ·

· EPI · NICOLAI · SERVACII · OARTINI · BENEDICT · ABBIS · EGIDII · OARIE ·

· OAGDALENE · AGATҺE · O͂ RIS · TҺEODERICVS · ABBAS · ҺI͂ D · EDIT ·

SCS PETRVS

SCS ANDREAS

SCS STEPHANVS

SCS LAVRENTIVS

THEODRICVS ABBAS II FIECIT

fabric that dates from as early as the ninth or tenth century [fig. 49]. Benedict is one of forty saints named in an inscription on the reverse of the altar whose relics were contained in a cavity beneath the central stone. Almost all of the relics are tiny fragments of bone, apart from the hair of St John the Evangelist and a semi-precious stone labelled as a relic of St Christopher.

The portable altar demonstrates at a glance the wide-ranging artistic talent that was employed to create sacred art in the Middle Ages. It consists of a wooden core with its centre hollowed out to receive the relics. Above this, resting on a recessed ledge, was placed the altar stone – the single most important component [fig. 48]. It was the altar stone that received blessing from the bishop and carried the power of consecration with it, allowing the liturgy to be celebrated outside the confines of a consecrated church. Although portable altars were endowed with relics from an early period, it was the Seventh Ecumenical Council of Nicaea in 787 that transformed custom into doctrine with the decree that all altars were required to contain the relics of saints in order to qualify for consecration. Exotic stones such as porphyry, serpentine, onyx, jasper and marble were the favoured materials for altars, selected for their preciousness and in reference to Old Testament descriptions. The stone at the centre of the Hildesheim portable altar is, in fact, a sedentary shelly limestone that was chosen for its convincing resemblance to porphyry. It is set into an engraved surround of gilt copper alloy, with roundels depicting the four symbols of the Evangelists at each corner and the figures of St Peter, St Stephen, St Andrew and St Laurence to the left and right. Also set into the surround are two ivories, the Crucifixion

Fig. 49
Portable altar (the relics)
See figs 47 and 48

When the altar stone is removed, a central
cavity is revealed which is stocked with relics
(above). The relic of St Benedict (right) is
wrapped in a Byzantine textile from the 9th
or 10th century that predates the altar.

The British Museum, London

Fig. 50
Enamel plaque
Northern France, *c.* 1170–80
Copper gilt, enamel, 10.9 x 4.9 cm

Probably from a small shrine or portable altar, this figure of St James would have formed part of a group of twelve apostles.

The British Museum, London

at the top, and the Virgin and Child with two bishop saints at the bottom. At each side there are two panels of manuscript illumination beneath rock-crystal covers, which depict and name, on the left, St Bernard of Hildesheim and, on the right, St Godehard, both of whom had shrines at Hildesheim. The same bishops are probably represented in the ivory with the Virgin and Child, where, however, they lack an identifying inscription. Importantly, the altar carries another inscription relating to its commission that reads: 'Thidericvs: Abbas: III: Dedit' ('Abbot Theodoric III gave it'). The third abbot Theodoric was the abbot of Godehardiklosters at Hildesheim between 1181 and 1204.

Master goldsmiths of the Meuse Valley

Patrons and artists alike might attach their names to their work, though the practice was by no means universal. Hugo d'Oignies, a lay brother of the monastery of St Nicholas at Oignies near Namur in present-day Belgium, is one of the better-known goldsmiths of the medieval age. His practice of signing his works has helped scholars to piece together a substantial body of material attributable to him and his workshop. His status as a wealthy goldsmith is self-consciously advertised on a pair of lavish book covers that he produced and gifted to the monastery between about 1228 and 1230. Hugo engraved an image of himself on a silver plaque presenting the book to St Nicholas. An inscription, meanwhile, identified him as the artist. He combined a breathtaking variety of techniques – often in the creation of a single object – and is duly recognized as one of the foremost goldsmiths of the thirteenth century.

Fig. 51
Reliquary of the rib of St Peter
Hugo d'Oignies
Namur, 1238
Silver gilt, bronze gilt, niello, gems, topaz,
garnet, beryl, pearls, rock crystal
50.5 x 35 cm

Musée provincial des arts anciens Namurois,
Namur

A strip of parchment contained within the relic compartment of the reliquary of the rib of St Peter ascribes this work to Hugo, too, dating the insertion of the relics to 1238 [fig. 51]. The reliquary is of a type often termed a 'speaking reliquary' because its shape is fashioned to reflect the relic that it contains. In many instances, the correlation between shape and content cannot be entirely taken for granted. The head of St Eustace, for instance, was the repository for many relics and not only the skull fragments that the head would seem to advertise. In this example, however, Hugo exploited the form of the reliquary perfectly to 'speak' its contents, although the rib fragment is not encased in the curved part of the reliquary that evokes the body part, but displayed in a rock-crystal cylinder that emerges from the centre of the 'rib' which is mounted on a pedestal. The application of filigree enlivens the curved surface of the reliquary, which is set with pearls, topaz, garnet, beryl and rock crystal. On the reverse, silver plaques inlaid with niello (an oxide of silver that turns black) carry a Latin inscription that explains: 'This vessel contains the rib of St Peter'.

Hugo d'Oignies was working geographically in a historic centre of excellence for medieval goldsmiths. The Meuse Valley takes into its sweep parts of northern France, Belgium and Germany, and during the Middle Ages constituted a region rich in natural resources for metalworking and enamelling. A number of prestigious ecclesiastical foundations provided sufficient patronage to ensure a golden age of productivity.

The best goldsmiths combined a number of different technical features in their works. The unknown artist of the gable-end reliquary

Figs 52 & 53
Two gable-end reliquaries
from the shrine of St Oda, Amay
Belgium, 11th and 12th centuries
Silver, silver gilt, copper, enamel,
rock crystal, horn
Fig. 52 below: 58.5 x 38 x 5.6 cm
Fig. 53 right: 58.3 x 38 x 6.5 cm

Walters Art Museum, Baltimore
The British Museum, London

with St Oda uses repoussé figures set within an internal border of
stamped silver-gilt metal sheets and an outer border decorated with
gilt copper alloy enamelled plaques [fig. 53]. The outer border is
punctuated with settings containing rock crystals at equidistant points
around the frame. The most precious part of the composition is, of
course, the relic content, which is arranged around the inner border.
Each compartment is equipped with the relics of female saints,
including the Virgin Mary, Mary Magdalene, the eleven thousand
virgin companions of St Ursula and Elizabeth of Thuringia. In the
centre stands the figure of St Oda, whose cult was focused at Amay
in Belgium. To either side of her are personifications of Religion
(left) and Almsgiving (right), qualities with which she was particularly
associated. Each is identified by an inscription. Panels of *vernis brun*,
a type of brown varnish with gold scroll work, create warmth and
variety on the hem of St Oda's gown, her sleeves and waist, and
the same treatment characterizes the haloes of all three figures. The
shape and composition of the reliquary suggests that it was originally
intended to form part of a twelfth-century house-shaped shrine to
St Oda. However, at some point between its completion around 1170
and the canonization of St Elizabeth of Thuringia in 1236, the ends of
the shrine were taken away and converted into independent reliquaries.
A corresponding end, probably from the same shrine, shows a figure
of Christ trampling on the lion and the serpent [fig. 52]. This scene is
taken from Psalm 90:13: 'You will tread on the asp and basilisk, the
young lion and the serpent you will trample underfoot', which was
taken as a symbol of Christ's triumph over death.

Fig. 54
Casket reliquary of St Valérie
Limoges, France, *c.* 1170
Copper gilt, enamel
16.5 x 29.2 cm

The British Museum, London

Limoges enamel

The metalworkers and enamellers of the Meuse Valley found themselves increasingly unable to compete with the emerging workshops of Limoges during the course of the first half of the thirteenth century. Limoges products were frequently infused with a degree of dramatic representation that appealed to popular taste. The legend of St Valérie, the patron saint of Limoges, decorates a number of caskets that combine elements of civic identity with religious understanding [fig. 54]. Her story relates how, upon her conversion to Christianity, she rejects her betrothed, Stephen, in favour of dedicating her virginity to Christ. Stephen's response to the news is predictably brutal and St Valérie is condemned to death by beheading. When the executioner strikes the blow, however, St Valérie catches her own head in her arms and walks away to seek the blessing of St Martial. Subtle elements of psychology are introduced into the narrative, particularly evident in the contrasting pose of Stephen on the front panel of the reliquary where he issues judgement against Valérie with all the energy of a rejected lover, compared with the reflective attitude he strikes on the lid when he receives the news of the miracle.

Opus lemovicense, the Latin for 'Limoges work', became the generally accepted term to describe all champlevé enamel wherever it was made, so great was the dominance of Limoges over enamel production. The workshop industry was prolific in its output, stimulated by the patronage that was offered by monasteries, bishops and, potentially, the English royal family. At this time, Limoges formed part of the English territories in France, and England no doubt provided

Fig. 55
Casket reliquary of St Thomas Becket
Limoges, France, c. 1190
Copper gilt, enamel, 15.5 x 21 cm

The Society of Antiquaries, London

a ready market, particularly for caskets commemorating the fate of
Thomas Becket (see pp.37–43).

Becket's murder inspired the designs of a large number of casket
or châsse (box) reliquaries – around fifty châsses or their fragments
survive today, probably a small proportion of the numbers originally
produced. It is by no means certain that the Becket châsses were
intended exclusively for the saint's relics: some may have been made
as reliquaries simply with scenes of Christendom's most topical and
popular saint to contain an assortment of different relics. However,
the fostering of Becket's cult in countries that experienced Plantagenet
marriages was most probably dependent on the circulation of his relics,
which appear to have been more accessible prior to the translation of
his body from the crypt at Canterbury Cathedral to a magnificent
new shrine at the east end in 1220. When Henry II's daughter Joanna
married William the Good of Sicily in 1177, she may have taken relics
of Becket with her. It seems that William's mother, Queen Margaret
of Sicily, received at this time from Reginald FitzJocelyn, bishop of
Bath, a gold pendant reliquary containing tiny fragments of Becket's
bloodstained vestments, hood, cloak, belt, shoe and shirt now in the
Metropolitan Museum of Art, New York. More difficult to argue,
perhaps, is a Plantagenet connection with the reliquary from the
Society of Antiquaries for London [fig. 55]. This impressive châsse,
which has lost its wooden core and the crest that would have
ornamented the roof, was discovered in Naples by the antiquarian
William Hamilton, and it has been speculated that it found its way
to Italy at the time of Joanna's marriage.

Fig. 56
Casket reliqury of the Magi
Limoges, France, *c.* 1250
Copper gilt, enamel, wood core
18.3 x 20.1 cm

The British Museum, London

Fig. 57
Flask reliquary
Flask: Egypt, 11th century
Mounts: Europe, 14th century
Silver gilt, rock crystal, niello
H 8.9 cm

The British Museum, London

Limoges benefited, too, from being strategically placed on the route to Santiago de Compostela (see p. 34). The volume of pilgrims passing through created a healthy customer base for the enamellers' sacred art. The movement of pilgrims from north to south between the major shrines of Cologne and Santiago de Compostela might conceivably account for the decision by the Limoges enamellers to capitalize on the cult of the three kings and produce beautiful châsse reliquaries with the Adoration of the Magi [fig. 56]. Each reliquary follows roughly the same compositional principles. The roof of the châsse shows the Magi following the star with some urgency on horseback, in contrast to the very measured pace that the Magi employ as they approach the Virgin Child, gingerly offering their gifts.

Making reliquaries: materials and influences

The materials considered appropriate to use in the manufacture of reliquaries were drawn from a long-established protocol governed largely by notions of purity. Gold, like the flesh of the saints, was considered to be incorruptible, and so gilt silver or gold were the most widely used metals in reliquary production. The application of enamel plaques to reliquaries, generally made from gilt copper alloy, or the construction of reliquaries entirely of enamel, as with the Limoges châsses, appears to have been acceptable presumably because of the quality of the workmanship and the precious appearance of their lustrous, glassy surfaces. A similar exemption was made for the use of Limoges chalices in the celebration of the mass in England despite stipulations by the Fourth Lateran Council

in 1215 that only gold or silver were suitable metals to receive the Eucharistic wine.

Other materials that were condoned include rock crystal and ivory. The transparency of rock crystal and its ability to magnify the contents of the material contained within it made it eminently desirable as a component in reliquary construction. Many reliquaries utilized the natural qualities of rock crystal to make visible their relics. The Christian understanding of rock crystal, derived largely from both pagan classical and Muslim learning, saw the substance as a sort of petrified water representative of great purity. The book of Revelation (22:1) reinforced this interpretation: 'And he showed me a pure river of water of life, clear as crystal, proceeding out of the throne of God and of the Lamb'. Rock crystal might be used as the relic chamber in a larger reliquary (see fig. 51) or as a spectacular means of magnification (see fig. 42), but it was also used as a reliquary vessel in its own right, perhaps enhanced with mounts. Henry III's relic of the Holy Blood (see p. 52) arrived in a crystal reliquary that in all probability was converted from a Fatimid bottle. Rock-crystal carving was a skill particularly enjoyed by Muslim craftsmen and there seems to have been no reluctance to convert their handiwork to Christian use. A small perfume bottle from Fatimid Egypt, dating possibly from as early as the eleventh century, became a treasured Christian possession when it was used to receive the relic of a hair from the Virgin Mary [fig. 57]. The fourteenth-century silver-gilt mounts describe the sacred Christian content, while the Arabic inscription on the body of the bottle extends: 'Blessing to its owner'.

Fig. 58
The Franks Casket
England, early 8th century
Whale bone, 13 x 23 x 19 cm

The British Museum, London

The incorporation of non-Christian elements into the design of sacred containers and reliquaries is exemplified most strikingly by the British Museum's Franks Casket, which dates from early eighth-century England [figs 58 and 59]. Although one of the principal scenes on the front of the box, the Adoration of the Magi, secures for it a Christian context, the remainder of the scenes that decorate it are a confusing mix drawn from Roman, Jewish and Germanic traditions. Each aspect of its narrative scheme is almost certainly, however, meant to reflect on Christian virtues. Consequently the gruesome story of Weland's revenge that is placed next to the Adoration of the Magi helps to illustrate models of good and bad kingship by juxtaposing Christ with the unjust King Nithhad. Weland, imprisoned by the tyrannical Nithhad, escapes to exact his revenge by murdering the king's two sons and raping his daughter. Despite the terrible nature of these acts, Weland's story demonstrates the ramifications of the rule of a bad king, Nithhad, as opposed to the ideal of Christian sovereignty exemplified by Christ.

The Franks Casket was made not as a reliquary but possibly as a box to store a holy text such as a Gospel or the Psalms. However, it appears that it may have been converted into a reliquary in the later Middle Ages when it was linked to the cult of St Julian at Brioude in the Auvergne. Its adaptation into a reliquary would have been determined by the fact that, although made of whale bone, it resembles ivory. Ivory, like gold and the flesh of the saints, was considered to be incorruptible.

The materials used in the fabrication of reliquaries were fundamentally important in the way that the power and mystique of relics were communicated to the devout. Relics were made more

visually appealing by their exterior casing in silver and gold, and
by the application of filigree and precious or semi-precious stones.
These materials were, furthermore, themselves thought to have divine
qualities and the power to affect cures in their own right. Medieval
lapidaries itemized the medicinal benefits that could be derived from
different gems – the sapphire, for instance, reflected celestial values and
was used to chasten the spirit, cool the blood and remedy poor eyesight.
Relics were accommodated in works not only of great beauty but of
intrinsic power that served as a microcosm of heaven and earth.

This tightly integrated cosmology was significantly disrupted in the
early years of the sixteenth century by the combined force of religious
reformation and, up to a point, Renaissance thinking, both of which
led to a greater secularization of society. The period of intellectual
enlightenment that characterized the eighteenth century secured a greater
understanding of the nature of materials that divested the reliquary of
much of its spiritual power. It was no longer appropriate, for example,
to believe that sapphires, rubies and emeralds emanated from the four
rivers of Paradise and provided a tangible link with the celestial realm.
Although the power of the relic itself was not diminished in the cultures
that still valued the intercession of the saints, its enrichment was
henceforth almost entirely a materialistic exercise. From the nineteenth
century onwards, the virtuosity and sheer beauty of the reliquaries
produced in the Middle Ages secured for them a secular audience of the
connoisseur and the curious. In terms of the contemporary experience, it
has frequently been remarked that museums, in many respects, represent
a secular parallel to the religious process of pilgrimage and veneration.

NOTES

1 'The Martyrdom of Polycarp' 18:2, in *The Apostolic Fathers: Greek texts and English translations of their writings*, translated by J.B. Lightfoot and J.R. Harmer. 2nd edn edited and revised by Michael W. Holmes (Grand Rapids Michigan, 1992).

2 'Plures efficimur, quoties metimur a vobis: semen est sanguis christianorum' from Tertullian, *Apologeticum* 50:13, in C. Baker, *Apologeticum. Verteidigung des Christendums* (Munich, 1961).

3 Gregory of Tours, *Glory of the Martyrs*, translated with an introduction by R. Van Dam (Liverpool, 1988), 9.

4 Ibid., 7.

5 D. Webb, *Pilgrims and Pilgrimage in the Medieval West* (London 2001), 26.

6 'E de la offerta fatta per gli pellegrini molto tresoro ne crebbe a la Chiesa e a' Romani: per le loro derrate furono tutti ricchi' from Giovanni Villani, *Nuova Chronica*, book 9, chapter 36, ed. G. Porta (Parma, 1991), vol. 2. Translated in Webb, op. cit., 117.

7 *The Book of Sainte Foy*, translated and edited by P. Sheingorn (University of Pennsylvania Press, 1995), 77.

8 Webb, op. cit., 23.

9 Ibid., 24.

10 Ibid., 79.

11 Holger A. Klein, 'Sacred Relics and Imperial Ceremonies at the Great Palace of Constantinople' in F.A. Bauer (ed.), *Visualisierungen von Herrschaft*, Byzas 5 (Istanbul, 2006), 79.

FURTHER READING

Barbara Baert, *A Heritage of Holy Wood: The legend of the True Cross in text and image* (Brill, Leiden and Boston, 2004)

Martina Bagnoli, Holger A. Klein, C. Griffith Mann and James Robinson, *Treasures of Heaven: Saints, relics and devotion in medieval Europe* (British Museum Press, London, 2011)

Debra J. Birch, *Pilgrimage to Rome in the Middle Ages* (Boydell Press, Woodbridge, 1998)

John Cherry, *The Holy Thorn Reliquary* (British Museum Press, London, 2010)

Raymond van Damm (ed.), *Gregory of Tours: Glory of the martyrs* (Liverpool University Press, 1988)

Timothy Husband (ed.), *The Treasury of Basel Cathedral* (The Metropolitan Museum of Art, New York, 2001)

Henk van Os, *The Way to Heaven: Relic veneration in the Middle Ages* (Amsterdam, 2000)

James Robinson, *Masterpieces: Medieval art* (British Museum Press, London, 2008)

Pamela Sheingorn (ed.), *The Book of Sainte Foy* (University of Pennsylvania Press, 1995)

Jonathan Sumption, *The Age of Pilgrimage: The medieval journey to god* (London, 2003)

Diana Webb, *Pilgrims and Pilgrimage in the Medieval West* (I.B. Tauris, London, 2001)

Leslie Webster, *The Franks Casket* (British Museum Press, London, 2011)

DVD/CD ROM

Pilgrims and Pilgrimage: Journey, spirituality and daily life through the centuries, interactive CD-ROM (1st edition: York, Christianity and Culture, 2007) ISBN 978-0-9550673-1-0

The English Parish Church through the Centuries: Daily life and spirituality, interactive DVD-ROM (1st edition: York, Christianity and Culture, 2010) ISBN 978-0-9550673-2-7

ILLUSTRATION ACKNOWLEDGEMENTS

All objects from the collection of the British Museum (BM) are © the Trustees of the British Museum. Further information about the objects and the collection can be found at www.britishmuseum.org.

Frontispiece: BM, The Waddesdon Bequest, PE WB67

Contents page: BM PE 1926,0409.1

p. 6 (map): with thanks to David Hoxley at Technical Art Services

Fig. 1: John Lawrence

Fig. 2: The National Gallery, London, NG4763, bought with contributions from The Art Fund, Benjamin Guinness and Lord Bearsted, 1934

pp.12–13: BM PE 1879,1220.1

Fig. 3: Capitulary Library of Vercelli, MS CLXV

Fig. 4: BM CM 1864,1128.194

Fig. 5: BM CM 1864,1128.195

Fig. 6: The British Library Board, BL Add. 28681, fol.9

Fig. 7: age fotostock/Robert Harding

Fig. 8: BM PE 1965,0604.1

Fig. 9 and Fig. 10 (left): BM PE 1856,0718.1

Fig. 10 (right): Kunstgewerbemuseum, Staatliche Museen zu Berlin, 1973,187-189 (photo. Bildarchiv Preussischer Kulturbesitz)

Fig. 11: BM PE 1882,0510.51

Fig. 12: BM PE 1879,1220.1

Fig. 13: BM PD 1904,0206.2.8

Fig. 14: BM PE 1855,0625.16

Fig. 15: BM PE 1855,0625.32

Fig. 16: BM PD E,1.87

Fig. 17: BM PD 1860,0414.230

Fig. 18: BM PD 1909,0612.14

Fig. 19: Photo. The Metropolitan Museum of Art/Art Resource/Scala, Florence

Fig. 20: © INTERFOTO / Alamy

Fig. 21: The British Library Board, BL Cotton MS Claudius BII fol.341r

Fig. 22: BM PE 1921,0216.62

Fig. 23: BM PE 2001,0702.1

p. 44: BM PE 1902,0210.1

Fig. 24: BM PD 1904,0206.2.2.

Fig. 25: Procuratoria della Basilica di San Marco, Venice (Santaurio 159)

Fig. 26: © F1 ONLINE / SuperStock

Fig. 27: Corpus Christi College, Cambridge, The Parker Library, MS16, fol. 216r

Fig. 28: BM PD 1895,0915.95.

Fig. 29: BM PE 1902,0210.1

Figs 30–31: BM, The Waddesdon Bequest, PE WB67

Fig. 32: BM PE AF.2765

Fig. 33: Photo: Vincent Leduc. Authors Image/Robert Harding

Fig. 34: BM PD 1933,0102.1

Fig. 35: BM PD 1911,0708.1

Fig. 36: BM PD 1895,0122.698

Fig. 37: BM ME 1959,0414.1

Fig. 38: BM PD 1911,0708.1

Figs 39–40: BM PD 1895,0122.188-9

Figs 41–2: BM PE 1850,1127.1

p.78: BM PE 1917,0409.1

Fig. 43: BM PE 1946,0407.1

Figs 44–5: BM PE 1889,0902.22, 23

Fig. 46: BM PE 1926,0409.1

Figs 47–9: BM PE 1902,0625.1

Fig. 50: BM PE 1850,1126.1a

Fig. 51 Photo. © KIK-IRPA, Brussels

Fig. 52: The Walters Art Museum, Baltimore, 57.519

Fig. 53: BM PE 1978,0502.7

Fig. 54: BM, The Waddesdon Bequest, PE WB19

Fig. 55: Society of Antiquaries for London

Fig. 56: BM PE 1855,1201.8

Fig. 57: BM PE AF3129

Figs 58–9: BM PE 1867,0120.1

INDEX